COMFORT FOOD FOR BREAKUPS

ARSENAL PULP PRESS
VANCOUVER

COMFORT FOOD FOR BREAKUPS

The Memoir of a Hungry Girl

MARUSYA BOCIURKIW

COMFORT FOOD FOR BREAKUPS
Copyright © 2007 by Marusya Bociurkiw

All rights reserved. No part of this book may be reproduced or used in any form by any means—graphic, electronic or mechanical—without the prior written permission of the publisher, except by a reviewer, who may use brief excerpts in a review, or in the case of photocopying in Canada, a license from Access Copyright.

ARSENAL PULP PRESS
200 - 341 Water Street
Vancouver, BC
Canada V6B 1B8
arsenalpulp.com

The publisher gratefully acknowledges the support of the Canada Council for the Arts and the British Columbia Arts Council for its publishing program, the Government of Canada through the Book Publishing Industry Development Program, and the Government of British Columbia through the Book Publishing Tax Credit Program for its publishing activities.

Text and cover design by Shyla Seller
Front cover photograph by Robyn Mackenzie
Author photograph by Meredith Woods
Kitchen icons by czardases at *istockphoto.com*

Printed and bound in Canada

An earlier version of "Radishes and Salt" appeared in *Zeek* magazine.

Efforts have been made to locate copyright holders of source material wherever possible. The publisher welcomes hearing from any copyright holders of material used in this book who have not been contacted.

Library and Archives Canada Cataloguing in Publication:
Bociurkiw, Marusya
     Comfort food for breakups : the memoir of a hungry girl / Marusya Bociurkiw.

ISBN 1-55152-219-5

     1. Bociurkiw, Marusya. 2. Food—Psychological aspects. 3. Bociurkiw, Marusya—Family. 4. Cookery. 5. Authors, Canadian (English)—Biography. 6. Motion picture producers and directors—Canada—Biography. I. Title.

PS8553.O4Z463 2007   C818'.5409   C2007-900227-7

ISBN13 978-1-55152-219-7

Also by Marusya Bociurkiw:

The Woman Who Loved Airports
Halfway to the East
The Children of Mary

CONTENTS

ACKNOWLEDGMENTS

I am indebted to those who took time out of their busy lives to read the manuscript and offer detailed commentary: Carolyn Gammon, Penny Goldsmith, Judith Nicholson, and Lori Weidenhammer. Vera Bociurkiw, Taras Bociurkiw, and Lesya Lashuk offered commentary and correction in certain crucial places, and some recipes were provided by Sheena Gourlay and Terri Roberton. Other recipes were borrowed or adapted with permission from Savella Stechishin's *Traditional Ukrainian Cookery*, Molly Katzen's *The Moosewood Cookbook*, *recipezaar.com*, *astray.com/recipes*, and my mother's own recipe journal. Certain books are quoted, invoked, or paraphrased: Mikhail Bakhtin's *Rabelais and His World*, Dionne Brand's *A Map to the Door of No Return*, Jacques Derrida's *Spectres of Marx*, Madhur Jaffrey's *A Taste of the Far East*, Primo Levis's *Survival in Auschwitz*, and Irfan Orga's *Turkish Cooking*, as well as Freud's essay "The Uncanny." It should be noted at this point that some (but not all) of the names in this book have been changed, and that all inaccuracies of memory or ingredients are the responsibility of the author. Billie Carroll designed the food blog that serves as a kind of counterforce to this book (*recipesfortrouble.com*), and did so with her usual artistry. I am also grateful for initial encouragement from Beth Macauley, and for funding from the Ontario Arts Council Writers Reserve program. Thanks also go to the energetic staff of Arsenal Pulp Press, and especially to Brian Lam who edited this book with sensitivity and elegance.

As with every book, there were people who provided respite along the way, via hospitality, meals, stimulating conversation, and supportive feedback. This list is too long too fully enumerate, but it must be said that Glen and Jeanette's exquisitely proffered oysters and cocktails on the shores of Fanny Bay, Lesya's heavenly Easter bread, Haida's orange chocolate birthday cake, Michael's delicious selection of British Columbia wines, Penny's French toast cooked up the day I left Vancouver, Jane's mushroom soup seasoned with family stories, and Margaret's Medusa-like production of three-course meals in the tiniest kitchen ever, gave the writing of this book its reason for being. Laurie Bell allowed me to cook for her, and provided a serendipitous gift of sensuality and affection during the final stages of this project.

Finally, I am deeply grateful to my mother Vera, not just for the delicious food and spicy anecdotes that have provided a life-long lesson in ways of moving pleasurably and graciously in the world, but also for the many times she listened to drafts of these stories: sometimes humming with pleasure, other times interrupting with caustic commentary. During those long afternoons of reading, eating, and textual analysis we agreed to disagree on how a family story or a cultural history may be told. Still, I recall that we did so with passion and orneriness—and above all, with love.

For my mother Vera,
who feeds me

PREFACE
Hungry Girl

You arrive at her house, matching Samsonite luggage at your side, or army surplus knapsack drooping off one shoulder: from the Edmonton airport, or the Greyhound bus station, or from hitchhiking across Canada. It could be ten a.m., or it could be midnight. But as soon as you get to the porch of her squat stucco bungalow on 111th Avenue, her reaction is always the same: matter-of-fact, fatalistic, even:

"*Nu.* You're here."

You're kissed profusely on both cheeks, immediately led by hand into the kitchen, and pushed into a chair (rather brusquely) at the head of a yellow formica table. Then, without much conversation, Evhenia Wasylyshyn, née Protskiv, born in a small village in Western Ukraine in 1903, and long since exiled to Edmonton, will get to work. No way are you allowed to help. She hauls foil-wrapped pots from the fridge and beat-up roaster pans from the back porch, fires up the gas stove, and brings platters of food to the table in the rhythmic, economic slow-shuffle she's perfected.

And then, no matter what the time of day or night, the eating begins. You roll up your sleeves, take a deep breath. You chew and swallow, chew and swallow, pacing yourself, knowing it's your solemn duty to ingest as much as you can: perogies, cabbage rolls, chicken stew, roast beef, and a Black Forest cake from Safeway for dessert, the kind with the plastic protective bubble. It's uncanny, the way she always has one of those cakes on hand, but you knew better than to ask questions.

Only after I've consumed several helpings does my grandmother sit down, Brown Betty teapot at her side, hands gently plucking the air as she talks. She's wearing a pretty chartreuse blouse she's sewn herself, a faded, pilly, navy blue sweater vest with a heraldic crest on the pocket, and a small burgundy blanket safety-pinned around her hips for extra warmth, brown polyester pants beneath. She has soft round apple cheeks, a girlish giggle, and a deep vein of bitterness that hardly anyone knows is there. I listen contentedly to sinister tales heard a hundred times before, told in a voice as mellow as tea: Baba's aged in-laws in Ukraine who, ever since the Berlin Wall came down, have been working the black market, smuggling VCRs and blue jeans into Kyiv; or the scary one about the cousin from the village, mysteriously shot dead, the day he was to leave for Canada. Food and stories, stories and food: it's a marathon, and you have to be prepared. It is painful, and deeply satisfying. Just as I've eaten far more perogies than I'd planned, Baba cunningly refills my plate. Trust me: I was never, ever hungry at Baba's.

Food doesn't always appear in the form of a meal on the table. Sometimes, it's a smell that shows up; at other times, it's not the meal I'm consuming, but an idea, or a recipe, or a gesture towards it, which feeds my hunger just the same.

Baba died a few years ago at age ninety-two, but the aroma of her kitchen—cabbage, garlic, onions frying in butter—is still in my nostrils. Sometimes I go to visit my mother and I'll be hungry, but for what, I don't know; maybe that crazy thing I've always wanted: family and lover, kin and skin. I walk into my mother's kitchen, alone, and there's that smell; there's my mother, bending over the stove and delicately picking perogies out of the boiling water, with the same anxious bend of back as Baba and those same swift, graceful hand movements, like something from an old fast-motion silent film. She's on her way to church, making sure lunch will be ready when she gets back: she's wearing a brightly coloured dress that's perfectly accessorized with scarf, earrings, and shoes, just like Baba taught her to do. My mind becomes a swath of celluloid, absorbing images, breathing light. My plate gets piled with too much food, and the stories—and occasionally arguments, too—begin.

Sometimes there are no recipes, just ingredients. Year after year, they reappear in my fridge and my cupboards, and I hardly know how they got there.

My father always accompanied my mother to the market on Saturdays, trailing after her and making a nuisance of himself, making sure she bought the foods he liked: smelly cheese, pickled herrings, heavy rye bread. Sometimes I came along, too: I loved the knowledgeable, conspiratorial way my parents conversed with the butcher, like they were plotting to overthrow the government instead of just buying pork hocks; I was fascinated by my father's reverent supplication at the cheese counter, confessing his lascivious need for Stilton and Roquefort.

My father the epicure, the brooding European intellectual, the trauma of war like blood in his eyes. He was the one who woke us up for school each morning, poking his head in the room and bellowing, "*Raus!*," German for "Out!" It wasn't exactly a Hallmark moment; still, we knew a hearty breakfast was imminent. In spring or summer, we'd come downstairs to watch the mad professor counting out strawberries into six separate bowls of cereal with demented, scientific precision. On winter mornings he'd be standing at the stove in his well-worn plaid woollen bathrobe, doling out buckwheat kasha or soft-boiling eggs with great dignity, as though preparing a keynote speech. He always served up the eggs in colourful carved wooden eggcups from the old country, buttered rye toast on the side. With my father, every meal was a ceremony, every food item full of intention and history.

My father, a career academic, was always leaving, flying off to scholarly conferences, then coming home with photos of places we didn't recognize. There was always a suitcase being emptied, or being filled; always, a sad, faraway look in his eyes. "But why was it always *Tato* who made us breakfast?" I asked my mother recently as we made perogies together. It was a few years after he'd died, and memories were coming back to us like pieces of mail returned to sender. "That was his idea," she sighed. "That was a time he wanted to himself, to spend with all of you." (Where was my mother at that time? In the basement, sorting laundry? In bed, reading novels and eating bonbons? I forgot to ask her.) Like the jar of pickled herrings I always keep at the back of the fridge, or the bag of kasha that's been in the cupboard, untouched for years, some memories offer a sudden, random comfort just by being there. I keep a memory of my father in the back of my mind: that portly man in PJs and bathrobe, serving breakfast with scholarly mien. I pull out the pickled herrings furtively late at night and eat them standing at the counter, accompanied by rye bread slathered with butter, the way *Tato* did.

Love doesn't always appear in a form you recognize. My friends and lovers are family, too; sometimes the meals they cook nourish me more than even Baba's endless feasts.

I am my family's self-appointed bearer of memory, recalling the absent spaces, recording the recipes, searching for the glimmer of devotion, the aroma of happiness, the back beat of bitterness. Between recipes and stories, I will ask myself a thousand times: who owns these memories? How is it that each of us remembers in a different way? If my way of remembering makes it to print, what does it do to theirs?

My recipe journals are full of histories long and short:

a grilled vegetable couscous with harissa sauce prepared the night my lover Krys first entered my kitchen; a marinara sauce that healed the wounds of a friend's breakup; my mother's perogy recipe, scrawled on the back of a brown paper Starbucks bag, because we were at the airport and it had been a difficult visit, and this exchange of culinary ephemera was the moment when we finally connected.

The pages of my cookbooks are a palimpsest, layered with notes and food stains, and the complex flavours of love and loss. It might take years for me to cook up that kasha, and I may prepare it differently, and for dinner instead of for breakfast. I might add eggs and onions, mushrooms and bow tie pasta; it will remind me as much of a favourite Ukrainian–Jewish restaurant in New York, as it will of my father. However I cook it, it will be the gesture of making it, as much as the food itself, that feeds the hungry girl inside of me.

KASHA VARNISHKES

Varnishkes is Yiddish for farfelle, or bow tie noodles. The origins of this dish are in dispute: did it originate from a recipe on the side of a box of kasha? Was it once a form of kreplach *(dumpling) stuffed with kasha? Was it born in the American diaspora or among the Ashkenazi Jews of Eastern Europe? No matter: it is a deeply satisfying dish, and highly nutritious.*

½ pkg (about 225 grams) bow tie pasta
¾ cup dried kasha, coarse grain
2 eggs
3 tbsp butter
2 onions, chopped
2 cloves garlic, smashed
1½ cups button mushrooms, chopped
3 cups chicken broth
Ladleful of pasta water
Salt and pepper to taste

In a large pot of boiling water, cook pasta according to package instructions as you assemble the rest of the dish. In a small bowl, mix kasha with beaten eggs and set aside. In a skillet on medium-high heat, brown onions and garlic in butter until soft and somewhat caramelized. Add mushrooms and sauté until soft, about five more minutes. Add kasha and cook, separating grains until slightly toasted. Add broth, pasta water, and salt and pepper. Bring to boil, then cover and simmer until broth is absorbed, about 20–30 minutes (kasha should be soft, but with a bit of a bite). Mix in cooked pasta. Season with additional salt and pepper. (This dish is also delicious with freshly grated Parmesan cheese, but it is rather untraditional to do so!) Can be served with mushroom sauce.

MAMA'S KITCHEN AND BEYOND

In East European cultures, appetizers are called *perekusky*. They can range from an elaborate buffet of pickled vegetables and smoked fish, cold meats and savoury pastries, to a few treasured dishes passed around the living room before dinner. My mother was famous for her *perekusky*, especially her canapés.

The 1960s were a sociable time for my parents. Against a backdrop of Vietnam on the television news and the Beatles on *Ed Sullivan*, my parents reinvented the cocktail party. They offered an excessive, theatrical display of hospitality for the legions of professors and their wives (I recall almost no female academics) who regularly swept through our living room, the men in tweed suits, the wives in little black cocktail dresses. For them, it must have been a bit like entering a European salon: the walls covered in oil paintings, the tables arrayed with embroidered cloths. My father in suit and tie, kissing the ladies' hands, helping them off with their coats and stoles; my mother, dark hair in an updo, dressed in a gorgeous silk frock Baba had made for her, blushing at some professor's lavish flattery. My father would sit the guests down and then, bending forward slightly in a kind of half-bow, would ask, "Can I offer you anything?" If the question was in Ukrainian, the guest would respond, ritually, by saying, "Whatever is plentiful in the house." This would give my father the opportunity to list all the numerous aperitifs, digestifs, wines, and spirits at the guests' disposal. Even as a child, I marveled at the measured formality of this exchange.

Meanwhile, hidden from view in the kitchen, the professor's children, some of us in flannel pyjamas, were lined up at the kitchen table, creating canapés via assembly line. There was a tense silence as my mother sliced the loaves of French bread and my brother created paper-thin slices of radish. Sweet pickles, cheese slices, and cold cuts were stacked within easy reach. Butter the bread, pass it on. Roll a slice of ham, place it on the bread, pass it on. Grab a swig of Coca-Cola in between. And so on, until all the ingredients were used up. My mother placed the canapés on a silver serving tray, and one of us would be assigned the task of carrying it out to the guests. I personally hated that job. Childless ladies with blonde helmet-hair towered over me, asking me questions too babyish for my age. Professors with goatees and liquor on their breaths leaned in too close. I preferred to keep a safe distance, peeking through the slats in the louvred doors.

My father was an academic for over forty years. Not long after arriving in Canada as a postwar refugee, and notwithstanding a year in a Nazi concentration camp, he quickly found himself a wife and applied to graduate school. Five children and two graduate degrees followed. The relentless grind of coursework, the tinny chaos of student housing, and the persistent, untidy exigencies of living with (if not actually raising) small children must have been overwhelming, but somehow comforting, for that political-prisoner-turned-student. During those workaholic postwar years, my father managed to lock away traumatic memories of an infamous hard labour camp called Flossenberg in Bavaria, Germany. It was only upon retirement that those terrifying images began to flicker in his memory once again.

Memory is cyclical, not linear. Certain seasons of life activate particular mental images and ways of remembering. When I visit Teresa, my graduate supervisor, I am taken back to my father's disheveled university office. We children loved to go there, certain that there would always be cookies in the lower-left-hand drawer of his desk, and, on the window sill, the primitive makings of tea. Gazing, for an absent, unguarded moment into the amber welcome of Teresa's ginger tea, I can almost see my father's brackish office brew, grey with powdered creamer. I can smell the chocolate-covered digestive biscuits overlaid with the mustiness of hundreds of books. I can feel the ambience of neglect: of one's children; of one's students; of one's very soul.

It's late fall in Vancouver, halfway into the first decade of the twenty-first century. I've defended and handed in my doctoral dissertation, have celebrated with friends. But now I must face fall convocation. I feel unequal to the task of performing this ritual for my mother, who will soon arrive to attend the ceremony. By the time my father got his PhD, he had a wife and two children. I am childless—just like those helmet-haired ladies from long ago—and single again, and, oddly, this perturbs me to no end. I develop an intense craving for my mother's *perekusky*. I invite several friends over for an after-party—appetizers and Veuve Cliquot—and ask my mother to be in charge of the food. Thus, the morning before convocation finds us at the Granville Island Public Market, my seventy-five-year-old mother's brow furrowed in concentration as she examines baguettes and cold cuts with suspicion, anxiously adding to the menu as we go along. We spend the rest of the day in the kitchen. My mother is the boss. Once again I am rolling slices of ham, slicing radish very thin, all according to my mother's exact specifications. At convocation, my mother bursts into tears at the sight of me in doctoral robes. My friend Joanna takes a photo. *Snap*: Me in burgundy robe and a wide-brimmed hat with gold tassel, smiling beatifically; my mother slightly behind me, white hair gleaming. We are illuminated, have haloes—saints in a Byzantine icon. My father lurks in the shadows, but on that day, I am my mother's daughter.

The cool autumn day ends with friends arriving at my door. This time, it is my mother who passes the canapés around.

RADISHES AND SALT

All I remember is this: a bakery that, for one night a week, was back-to-front: the storefront dark and unpeopled, the back brightly lit as though for a party. I remember that we seemed to be a chosen few—my father with two or three children in tow, and a handful of other anointed disciples. Pastry aficionados, all of us, with the good fortune to be in the confidence of a bald, deep-voiced Jew whose name escapes me, the proprietor of the Bon Ton Bakery in Edmonton, whose Saturday night sales we were privy to.

I can see this in my mind's eye: impossibly wide trays of prune-filled *hamantaschan* and crisp, heart-shaped *palmier,* covering long, scarred wooden tables where dough was usually kneaded, rolled, cut, and basted. Tall racks filled with trays of oval-shaped poppyseed roll; loaves of crusty rye bread and shining *challah*; Dobosh torte, rum babas, *petit fours*, potato knishes. Items so deeply discounted that we children had the usually forbidden pleasure of choosing what we wanted for our own impractical desires—thus, gingerbread men, sugar cookies, and *rugaleh* could also be found in my father's stash.

The backroom of the Bon Ton Bakery smelled of dough and the overbearing sweetness of so many hours of yeast mingling with water, flour, sugar, and air, a deeply familiar scent that somehow also evoked long afternoons and mother's milk. But there were other, more deeply timbered, spicy smells that held within them a kind of secrecy and melancholy; a musky scent that marked this space and those of us in it, as anomalous amid the flat, snowy (in my memory there is always snow) prairie suburb. The essence of the foreigner caught in my nostrils, and with it, thirty-year-old memories of the *selo* and the *shtetl*, the horrors of war, the bittersweet relief of refuge in another country. My father's memories, my memories: when you're a child, you can hardly tell them apart. My father, in travelling so religiously, as though to a church or a *shul* to this bakery, was revisiting a site both *heimlich* and *unheimlich*; what Freud described as "that class of the frightening, which leads back to what is known of old and long familiar." The bakery was a hybrid location that both revealed and concealed. Perhaps it reminded my father of all that was good and terrible about growing up in a small town in a colonized country on the eve of war: the sharp pungency of rye and caraway, the gentle, forgiving aroma of egg bread, the honey cake's complex perfume.

My father came from a place and time that hated the Jew. Nonetheless, much daily barter in the depressed economy of early twentieth-century Ukraine depended upon the informal trade between the Jewish entrepreneur forbidden to hold land, and the land-rich, cash-poor Ukrainian farmer. War came, with all its horrors, shakily imprinted onto films and photographs, relived in nightmares and memories. Jews disappeared from the villages overnight. People didn't know why, and didn't ask; or knew, and didn't say. Ukraine bears a heavy burden of complicity with anti-Semitism; its history of pogroms has yet to be fully acknowledged and documented, let alone worked through. Unrecorded, too, are the alliances, the small solidarities, the meals and customs furtively exchanged amid terror. For there were also those who resisted and who, by doing so, risked their lives. My great aunt Olena, well into her nineties, told me recently that during World War II, she routinely hid Jews in her tiny house in Western Ukraine, and fed them a meal each night. When I asked her if she had been afraid, she snorted contemptuously—"When someone comes to your door hungry, you take them in, and you give them a meal. *That* is what you do."

What I don't remember about those Saturday nights at the Bon Ton Bakery is what comes up in conversation with my older brother Taras, years later. Taras says there were more than just a handful of people at the Saturday night Bon Ton Bakery sales; he says there were lineups of perhaps forty or fifty pastry fanatics, and that we children were strategically brought along so that, upon entering the backroom, we could fan out and grab the best booty. My brother tells me that he remembers the baker's tattoo—his number from the concentration camp. My father also spent time in a concentration camp, for resisting the German army as they encroached upon Ukraine. As far as the Nazis were concerned, Slavs were to be the next target, after the Jews. I ask Taras why my father didn't have a number, and he says he thinks it was because political prisoners, slightly higher up on the camp echelon, didn't get tattooed. (I find out later that only those at Auschwitz were tattooed.) We wonder if they ever talked about it, the baker and the professor, two concentration camp survivors from two different worlds.

What *I* remember is this: the brown, grease-stained paper bag of potato knishes we brought home along with the bread, the pastries, the cakes. My mother, who never came along with us to the bakery, would decry to my father the excesses of rum babas; and *why*, in the name of Jesus and Mary, did we need *three loaves* of pumpernickel bread? We kids nimbly stayed out of the line of fire; we quietly set the knishes onto a baking tray, put them into the oven to warm for five to ten minutes, and then snatched them off the tray as quickly as we could, savouring their moist flakiness and the slightly spicy pillow of potato filling inside. I always thought knishes were Ukrainian;

I confused them with the word for blood sausage, *kishka*, and the word for book, *knyzhka*, and in my mind all those things were related: food, blood, words.

What I have left is this: a meagre mental file of story fragments from my father, a man so deeply traumatized by the war and the camps, he was unable to talk about it fully until a few years before his death. And even then, it wasn't so much talk as a series of terribly sad gestures and words.

The storm of trauma began slowly, like an unsettling wind. *Tato* was in his late sixties by then. My father, usually so uninterested in domestic affairs, decided to rearrange my mother's china cabinet. My mother, highly perturbed by this incursion into her empire, sent him to bed for a nap. When he woke up, he thought my mother and I were Nazis, and decided to escape. He filled a small suitcase with a shirt and some ties, his Canadian passport and his driver's license. Then he went downstairs in his pyjamas and prepared a heartbreakingly simple meal to take on an imaginary train: radishes and salt, which he very carefully placed into a ziplock bag. He became extremely agitated, then aggressive. There was an ambulance, there were sedatives. There was, miraculously, a psychiatric intern who sat with my father for eight hours or more and heard all the stories we hadn't been told. Finally, a daily program of drugs was prescribed to contain the seemingly dangerous flood of memory. There was, for my father, no catharsis, no binding, no closure.

My father's suitcase had been light enough for sudden flight, but this would have been a journey *away* from the safety of a Canadian suburb, from aluminum-siding-clad homes guarding capacious refrigerators. This was a suitcase and a man ready, if only for a moment, to travel back to the past, to fabricate a return. This was my father's final, courageous attempt to reclaim memory, and my telling of it, a way to resolve my own uneasy recollection.

Once a week, on my way home from university in Vancouver, I enact a kind of ritual to celebrate the end of another weekly cycle of words and deadlines. I get off the bus at Broadway and Macdonald and make a beeline for Solly's Bakery, where I buy a week's worth of bagels and cream cheese, then linger for a while looking for just the right pastry—poppyseed cake, or *rugaleh*, a knish if I'm lucky enough to find one—that tastes and smells like, and unlike, home.

My father died a few years ago. Memory does its slow, necessary work. It is only very recently that I have been able to recall the pleasant memories from childhood, most of them connected to food. The kasha breakfasts my father made most winter mornings when we were kids, that gritty old-world smell wafting through the house. The pleasure of European cheeses and wines he taught me to appreciate when I was older: gewürztraminer, cabernet; havarti, gruyere, gorgonzola. The backroom of that bakery, the crisp astringent smell of Alberta winter transformed into the warm, rounded aromas of Eastern Europe, a portly Ukrainian professor and a bald, elegant Jewish baker nodding to each other over a transaction of knishes and history, a young girl looking on.

FRESH COFFEE

As a child, I loved to watch my mother's face when she ordered coffee in a restaurant. When the steaming cup arrived, she'd frown and blow on it suspiciously. The suspense was unbearable. She'd take a first, dainty sip, then sigh, deeply, sensually. *Dobra kava*, she'd say—good coffee. I'd sigh too, with relief. At the time, I had no idea why this bitter, unsweet liquid was so crucial to her happiness. But these days, I have my mother's same devotion to good coffee, and will search for it across cities and entire continents.

The coffee I had at Roxolana's apartment was an elegant, complicated, affair—the same words I would use to describe Kyiv, capital of Ukraine, in all of its social and architectural complexity. Mythical Kyiv, long ago the cultural centre of Eastern Europe, now a Stalinist makeover. Postcolonial Kyiv, surreal with ATMs, rickety high-rises, ubiquitous currency exchanges, and amputees begging on sidewalks. Cosmopolitan Kyiv, avenues lined with floridly blooming chestnut trees, punctuated with the solemn busts of poets, intercut with stores brassily selling Prada, Chanel, Dior. Imaginary Kyiv, mecca for Ukrainians who come from North America to find their roots, disappointment and hope etched on their faces, crumpled American dollars in their hands. Coffee was the least of it, but coffee would turn out to be something that would provide a pause, familiarity, a welcome site of reflection.

When I am travelling, coffee is the source of both my

greatest hope and greatest fear. I am dreadfully addicted it, and cannot function without it. How will I assure that it will be available, in rich steamy abundance, immediately upon my awakening? Will it offend my hosts in Berlin, or Prague, or Kyiv, if I bring my tiny Italian stove-top espresso maker, or my Melitta filter?

At Carolyn and Katharina's sunny, dishevelled apartment on Sorauer Strasse in Berlin, I am usually the first one up. I negotiate my way through last night's dishes and little Noel's picture books, trucks, and Peter Rabbit bowl, groping for the kettle, finding the Melitta filter lodged inside a saucepan. We drink the coffee with dense, brown German bread and gouda cheese before I head out to explore the carnival that is Kreuzberg, their neighbourhood on the border between what people there still refer to as east and west Berlin.

At Barb's apartment in downtown Prague, I can smell the coffee as I wake, always made in Barb's king-size espresso pot that she brought with her from Canada. Back in her Montreal bachelor days, warm milk was frothed with a handheld Braun blender, and we drank our coffee from bowls as we lounged on expansive couches like pashas. On this morning, I warm the milk myself, waiting for Barb to return from taking her daughter to school. Later, we will sit in a café on Stare Mesto Square, beneath the Old Town hall with its ornate astronomical clock, sipping frothy long espressos, eating croissants, talking dreamily, long and deep into the afternoon.

In preparation for my first trip to Ukraine, I bring coffee with me, thick, chocolaty grounds from a corner grocery store in Prague. I feel efficient and smug as I pack the shiny yellow package into my bag. Ukraine is a nation of tea drinkers, and my expectations are low.

My first morning in Kyiv is strange, watery: it's as though I am seeing everything through one of those old-fashioned glazed windows from a *noir* film: shadowy figures, indiscernible intentions. I am in the country where my parents were born, but it doesn't feel extraordinary enough to have warranted this long, uncomfortable journey. Instead, to my uninformed western vision, it's just an impoverished corner of Europe: vaguely familiar, utterly strange, just like Freud's notion of *unheimlich*. After the beautifully restored opulence of Prague, the squalor of Kyiv's inner city is a shock. There are shiny-suited Russian Mafioso everywhere—walking clichés wielding cell phones, big-haired Russian women on their arms. My thoughts take a paranoid turn. Does my cousin Roxolana, who is hosting me so generously, really like me, or does she just see me as a brutish westerner, stealing the soul of her country with my video camera?

I don't yet know that Roxolana normally stays up half the night and rarely breakfasts before noon. I haven't yet perceived her quiet, matter-of-fact graciousness, her open heart. In honour of the first day of my visit, she is dressed and groomed at the ungodly hour of nine o'clock. Two filo pastries lie primly on a saucer. There are strawberries in a blue bowl, there is thinly-sliced cheese on a wooden board. Sunlight filters in, antique gold, through the kitchen's tall, dusty windows. Roxolana is in the kitchen as I enter, spooning a goodly amount of the Czech coffee I brought into an improbably small hammered metal pot that looks vaguely Turkish to me. She adds water, almost to the brim, and then says that the coffee must be watched constantly until the merest indication of a boil. Later, when she runs to another room to answer a phone call, I choke back the coffee, grounds and all, poured directly from pot to cup, in what I think is a very good show of manners and etiquette.

I carry out this ritual for several days, on my own. Soon enough, however, I slip into a Kyivan routine of late dining and drinking. I meet people, am welcomed into their homes, whisked to queer bars, to cavernous restaurants and tiny basement cafés. I begin to see another side of Kyiv. I notice that there are street musicians everywhere, playing ancient melodies, on violin, on bandura, on accordion, singing in polyphonic harmony. I spend an afternoon with a Ukrainian male-to-female transsexual and her lesbian lover who met each other through the Internet. They offer me sweet buns, obtained at a kiosk on the street, and take none for themselves. Their genial, delicate hospitality, proffered amid small, crowded quarters, is a flavour I've never had: Ukrainian mixed with queer. In a sidewalk café off Independence Square, I taste the rounded, plummy essence of Georgian wine for the first time, in the company of new friends. I feel the warmth and softness of the spring air, inhale the aroma of flowering chestnut trees. Grudgingly, I begin to appreciate this noble, wounded city and to recognize its dour, irreverent people as my own.

On one of my last days in Kyiv, Roxolana and I rise at the same time. We smile at each other in dazed, good-humoured recognition. By now we have spent many sociable hours together, smoking cigarettes, taking coffee, wandering along the avenues like Parisian *flâneurs*. Roxolana has said to me shyly, proudly, "We are like sisters." She makes the coffee that morning, and after the black tarrish blend has demurely bubbled, she pours it in a single graceful gesture through a tiny strainer into my cup. I manage to hide my surprise. Thick and smooth, it's the best cup of coffee I've ever had.

SUNDAY SOUP

On Sunday mornings, I wake up thinking about soup. I make an inventory of the refrigerator's contents, assessing the state of wilted carrots and remnants of celery, deciding on the kind of stock, trying to match the soup to my mood. More often than not, Sunday for me is a day for writing, and making soup provides a good release for artistic energies that have been brewing and stewing all day.

My earliest memory of soup is from Ukrainian summer camp in rural Alberta. It is also, perhaps, my first memory of injustice, felt with a child's razor-sharp sense of right and wrong. This was not a typical summer camp where canoeing lessons, craft sessions, and weenie roasts are the order of the day. This was Ukrainian girl scout camp, distant cousin to Brownies and Guides. Instead of sweetly gathering around toadstools, we did early morning military drills in front of flagpoles, learning to march in precise formation and turn corners sharply. I imagined us marching across the prairies of Alberta and Saskatchewan, traversing the rivers and lakes of Manitoba, passing by the Great Lakes and then crossing the ocean to Ukraine, where we would liberate our people from the dullness of Soviet apparel once and for all. But we were assigned no such glorious task. Each afternoon, we tramped several dusty miles to a lake, splashed desultorily in water full of leeches, and tramped back, an army of disappointed, obedient children.

The camp director was called *Kommandantka*, and even now, I can recall her shrill, needy voice. She was possessed of several chins and wore size ten shoes. She was always in uniform, even when no one else was, and her blouse was always perfectly pressed. Our Ukrainian elders at these camps had very little sense of measure or restraint. Years earlier, they had marched hungrily across entire countries, fleeing invaders, losing their youth along the way—only to find themselves in this ragged prairie acreage filled with skinny trembling aspens, rundown bunkhouses, and a muggy creek. Our rows of docile bodies, dressed in uniform for reveille, must have reminded them of the camps where they themselves had been interned. A longing for power, sensations of helplessness, and quick, flaming licks of anger must surely have competed with their devotion to us, the new generation growing up so innocently and ungratefully in a freer land.

There were many things we disliked about summer camp, from the thick yellow creek water we drank, rumoured to be full of boys' piss, to *Kommandantka's* meaningless angry commands, issuing forth from a mouth ringed with messy orange lipstick. But it was the food I despised most of all. It was plain and repetitive, and simply not fun: boiled eggs and bread for breakfast, soup for lunch, mushy stew for supper. There was never corn on the cob or cheeseburgers; exotic items like S'mores or ice cream were unheard of.

My friend Myroslava Mankowych was pretty and well-behaved, and detested pea soup as much as I did. She was the perfect foil, or so I thought. Myroslava and I soon worked out a neat system of dumping our meals behind a bush and later, delving into our top-secret stash of O'Henry bars, Twizzlers, and Coke. One particular, doomed day, pea soup was on the menu yet again: leaden, bland, and curiously grey. With a quick, silent glance at each other, Myroslava and I agreed to meet behind the dining hall. But *Kommandantka*, anticipating our revolt, had organized a stakeout, pouncing heavily and dramatically from behind a corner of the building the minute we bade our soup rations goodbye. We were reprimanded, loudly and severely. I was punished, though I can't remember how. Myroslava burst into tears but, to my chagrin, was spared any further repercussions, for her mother was one of the camp leaders, and a friend of *Kommandantka*'s. Then and there I lost any respect I might have had for *Kommandantka*'s authoritarianism and the camp's parsimonious ways. A lifetime of rebellion against authority was to follow.

Another early memory of soup I have is not unrelated. One of the few things my father ever told us about his experience as a political prisoner in a Nazi concentration camp was the soup. He told us that he was always hungry, and that the only thing he had to eat most days was potato peel soup: bland, unnourishing, and, we imagined, dirty too, full of bits of mud and shards of bark. We loved this story—which had, no doubt, been watered down for our childlike consumption. It made us shiver with a kind of revulsion mixed with a haughty sense of our own good fortune. But mostly, we loved how the story ended. My father was something of an artist, and he told us that the way he survived was to make drawings for the cook. The cook then gave him extra food which, presumably, he shared with the others. A simple equation: the drawings bought him more soup, the soup bought him life, and that life permitted us ours. Other historical accounts of the camps—Primo Levi's *Survival in Auschwitz*, in particular—corroborate the basic details of his story, with its gesturing to the desperate underground economy of camp culture. Having something to barter—a spoon, an extra bit of clothing—could mean the difference between life and death. I've never heard anything about artwork having currency in that traumatic environment, but perhaps that is my own failure of imagination. I used to wonder if my father made that part up; perhaps he traded more prosaic items with the cook (himself a prisoner), like a tin bowl, or a decent pair of shoes. According to Levi, sore feet were the worst thing that could happen in a hard labour camp. It seemed to me that it was a well-fitting pair of shoes, not art, that might permit one's survival. Apocryphal or not, I like the abject lesson that my father's story imparted: that art had the power to change people's minds; that it could not only make life livable but that it could, in fact, save lives.

Two things have stayed with me from that oft-repeated story. One is that I despise watery soups, thin bisques, or bouillions of any kind. The soups I make are solidly built, like my no-fail minestrone with its thick base of onion, garlic, olive oil, vegetable broth, and puréed tomato, its crowding together of beans, potatoes, eggplant, celery, and carrots, its generous sprinkling of Romano cheese. My squash soup is similarly no lightweight: one chopped, sautéed onion, an entire head of roasted garlic, and two or more cups of chicken broth combined with one roasted squash's orange purée, along with a half cup of yogurt or the juice of half a lemon, added at the last minute. On top of this I usually float shards of roasted red pepper, or a cup of sautéed oyster mushrooms, depending on my mood. In the middle of a cold Vancouver winter, when a fine grey mesh of rain surrounds the house and the mountains have long since disappeared into mist, I'll tackle the classic Portuguese peasant dish, *caldo verde*, where kale forms a comforting accord with mashed potatoes and spicy sausage.

The other message in my father's story is that artmaking is not to be taken lightly. In East European cultures, the vocation of artist is passed on in families, generation to generation. In Ukraine, no one blinks an eye if you say you're an artist; it's like saying you're a plumber or an engineer. People nod, satisfied. Nonetheless, my father gave up on his art career soon after the war and became an academic. It was to me he passed on his cumbersome wooden oil paint case, his compact metal watercolour box. These days, I find myself with one foot in academia and one in the world of artmaking. My Sunday soup is the hyphen between two parts of my life and history.

Soup can sometimes take the place of language, when words themselves curdle in a broth of strangeness and misrecognition. It's ten p.m. on a June Sunday evening in Kyiv. I come back to my cousin Roxolana's apartment, thinking we had a rendezvous, but we have missed each other and so, uneasily, I am there alone with Yaroslava, Roxolana's beautiful, formidable flatmate. Like almost everyone I will meet in Ukraine, Yaroslava has a shadow of tragedy that co-exists with a deep zest for life. Her husband died nine months earlier, of cancer. Yaroslava's grief has taken over the household; at breakfast, even in the middle of laughter, her kohl-rimmed eyes will cloud over, and she will rake her hands through her dark, dishevelled hair and begin to weep. Then the cloud passes as quickly as it came and she swiftly resumes chain-smoking her ultra-thin "Vogue" cigarettes, dispensing her clever, bitchy wit. Yaroslava's humour is caustic, a piquant stew of sorrow and bitterness. She and Roxolana will often break into peals of laughter at some grammatical malapropism I've innocently uttered in my patchwork Ukrainian. Roxolana's laughter is compassionate, but with Yaroslava, I sense a mocking undertone: the glint of metal, the sharpness of a steel trap. How silly we children of postwar refugees must appear to her: coming back, after all those years of simulacra, a copy with no original; returning to a homeland we have never seen, and about which we appear to have learned absolutely nothing.

But on that particular June night in Kyiv, Yaroslava is in a pensive, generous mood. The sky outside is the colour of eggplant, the air is soft as silk. It is *Zeleni Sviata*, the Green Season. Indeed, I have seen several people in the Metro with arms full of green branches, and all the churches are decorated with poplar fronds. *Zeleni Sviata* is meant to mark the Pentecost, but its roots are decidedly pagan, unfurling back to ancient rituals celebrating summer solstice. Yaroslava has just returned from church and, whether by coincidence or design, she has prepared a green borscht which she is eager to share with me. I protest, having already eaten dinner, but she ladles soup into a bowl anyway with that fierce, almost bullying hospitality so typical of Eastern Europe.

Green borscht has no beets in it; its primary ingredient is sorrel, a lemony-tasting herb which grows wild in Ukraine. Onions are fried in butter. Soup stock and chopped vegetables are added, cooked until tender, then strained. An abundance of chopped sorrel is then added to the broth along with a paste of sour cream and flour and chopped dill. The soup is customarily served over half a hard-boiled egg. The experience of eating it—which I savoured for the first and only time in Yaroslava's kitchen—is like inhaling a meadow in high summer: the feel of the earth, the aroma of green.

It is late, but outside the people of Kyiv are emerging onto the street, to stroll, to take coffee, to drink vodka or sip wine. No matter how small the budget or the meal, their gatherings will be ceremonious, celebratory. As Yaroslava anxiously chain-smokes and I eat soup, I get a sense of what I can only describe as Ukrainian soul: a spiritual and emotive depth that supersedes trauma, elevates it, mocks it, and, finally, makes soup out of it.

NO-FAIL MINESTRONE SOUP

This is one of those soups you can make on Sunday and eat all week. Its flavour improves with each passing day.

1 tbsp olive oil
1 medium onion, finely chopped
3 cloves garlic, minced
1 small eggplant, diced
4 carrots, chopped
2 cups cold water
1 can tomatoes or 6 or 7 large fresh tomatoes, diced
2 tbsp tomato paste
1 tsp salt
½ tsp pepper
1 tbsp oregano or basil, dried or fresh
handful fresh parsley, finely chopped
1 12-oz can kidney beans
2 potatoes, peeled and diced
handful fresh parsley, finely chopped (garnish)
½ cup grated Romano cheese (optional)

In a deep pot on medium, heat oil. Sauté onion, garlic, eggplant, and carrots until everything is tender. Add water, tomatoes, tomato paste, salt, pepper, and herbs, and slowly bring to a boil, stirring constantly. Lower heat and let simmer for approximately 20 minutes. Add kidney beans and potatoes and simmer on low heat for about another 20 minutes or until potatoes are cooked. Serve in soup bowls sprinkled with parsley and Romano cheese, some crusty bread on the side. Makes 6 servings.

TOMATOES

Biliana said that in the summer after the Chernobyl meltdown in Ukraine, the tomatoes were as big as grapefruits and as sweet as wine. She was living in Bulgaria at the time. She was a kid, and Bulgaria was still Communist then. The day of the meltdown dawned sunny and warm. A hike had been scheduled by the Pioneers, the young Communist group every Bulgarian child had to belong to. Despite the news, group leaders felt it would set a bad example if they cancelled, so Biliana and her fellow Pioneers marched dutifully through the hills as radioactive clouds bloomed on the horizon. They were a colourful sight, red kerchiefs on their necks, yellow snow falling on their shoulders.

My mother was never much of a gardener. The only vegetables that really ever turned out for her were tomatoes. Planted next to the pink gladiolas, they grew in near-grotesque profusion. All summer, we ate thickly sliced tomatoes sprinkled with chopped green onions and a simple vinaigrette, alongside the potato salad and the barbecued hamburgers. My mother's tomatoes required little else. At the end of summer she'd pick the green ones too so they wouldn't freeze, and they'd line every window sill in the house, an uneven display of lime-green orbs, a science experiment gone wrong. By fall, my mother was sick of tomatoes, so she'd just give them away to neighbours and friends, casually handing them over in bulging Safeway bags.

When we were little, we were shipped off to my grandmother's house for entire afternoons, and sometimes, if we were lucky, overnight too. My Baba religiously believed in letting kids do exactly as they please. On any given sunny Sunday afternoon we were allowed to sit in front of the television, a TV table placed conveniently in front of us. Unlike our parents, Baba would let us eat our meals right there in the living room while watching an afternoon movie—not only that, she'd *bring* the food to us, whatever we wanted. For me, it was always tomato sandwiches. Baba placed slices of tomato between pieces of white bread that had been lavishly spread with Hellman's mayonnaise. She'd salt the tomatoes, insert a layer of iceberg lettuce, slap the bread together, cut the sandwich into four triangles, and serve it with a root beer float. Those tomatoes, fruity and sweet, were fresh off Baba's vines.

About fifteen years ago, I travelled to Nicaragua with a group of activists. Nicaragua was still Socialist then, still free of *el Yanqui*, and governed by the idealistic, romantic Sandinista regime. Our earnest brigade of twenty or so artists, community organizers, and trade unionists went to a small village in the rural north to help pick coffee beans. I will never forget the cacophony of the roosters, accompanied by the syncopated beat of women's hands in the community kitchen as they slapped tortilla dough into rounds for breakfast. The first meal was charming: black beans, rice, and those light, freshly-made corn tortillas, which we seasoned with the hot sauces and condiments we'd brought along. But for the rest of the month, those same three items appeared at every single meal. We all lost weight, and learned what it means to eat food as fuel, divorced from novelty or pleasure, the way most of the world experiences it. We learnt *solidaridad*—solidarity—through our bodies, and not just our minds.

One morning, a member of our group had to go into town for medical attention. At the end of day, some of us ran into her on the road as she returned from Matagalpa. She had with her a brown paper bag full of knobby, pockmarked tomatoes, purchased in town, which she intended to share equally with our entire brigade. The five of us stood there, tired and dusty from a day in the fields, each allowed one democratic bite out of a single, fresh tomato. I remember how quiet and how reverent we were. Few things I've eaten since have had such impact on my tastebuds, something indescribably sweet and tender unfolding there.

Once, my Parisian friend Claire showed up unexpectedly at my door. "*C'est absolument fini*!" she proclaimed dramatically, sweeping one hand through the air as though tossing something away. She had just broken up with her girlfriend. Her usually elegantly styled hair was plastered to her head from walking in the rain. She had a bottle of wine under her arm, only half-full. What could I do but invite her for dinner? It must have been fall, because I had a basket of fresh tomatoes in my kitchen. I decided to make pasta sauce. I sat Claire down with a glass of her raunchy Italian wine, some tomatoes, and a chopping board. I busied myself with the other ingredients: onions, garlic, artichoke hearts, fresh basil and parsley. I put spaghetti on the boil.

We cooked up that sauce in no time, and Claire's Gallic temperament prevailed. She moved fluidly from sadness to anger to hilarity as I stirred the sauce and refilled her glass. Her hands were eloquent, waving back and forth as she described their final argument and all the passionate, brilliant things she'd said, or at least wished she had said. The sauce, which should simmer about half an hour, filled the room with its tart, jammy perfume. Dusk fell, and I turned on a lamp. We moved on to other topics: where we'd go hiking next weekend, and whether it's actually possible for Anglo-Saxon women to appreciate good food. I served up the spaghetti with a wedge of parmesan for grating on top, and slices of crusty sourdough bread from the Czech bakery around the corner. Amid the music of Claire's French accent, it felt like we could be in Paris, eating a cheap but fabulous bistro meal. But no, we were in Vancouver, it was starting to drizzle again, and you could catch a slight whiff of cedar through the open window. The North Shore mountains were a faint, slouching shadow along the horizon.

Claire went on to have many more affairs, as did I. I've lost touch with her but always think of her, and of broken hearts and new love, when I make this sauce.

PASTA SAUCE PASSIONATA

¼ cup olive oil
2 cups onions, chopped
4 cloves garlic, minced
½ tsp dried red pepper flakes, crushed
2 cups fresh tomatoes, chopped
¼ cup tomato paste
½ cup fresh parsley, finely chopped
½ tbsp dried oregano
salt and pepper to taste
1 6-oz jar marinated artichoke hearts, chopped
1 roasted red bell pepper, peeled and chopped
½ cup fresh basil, chopped
Parmesan cheese, grated

In a large saucepan, heat olive oil. Sauté onions, garlic, and red pepper flakes until onions are translucent. Add tomatoes, tomato paste, parsley, and oregano. Season with salt and pepper. Simmer, uncovered, over medium heat for about 20 minutes, or until somewhat reduced. Add artichoke hearts, as much juice as desired (depending how thin or how tangy you want the sauce to be), the chopped red pepper, and basil. Simmer for another 15 minutes. Serve over hot pasta, grating Parmesan cheese on top. Makes 4 servings.

EGGS

A scene from a nineteenth-century landscape painting unfolds outside the window of my taxi. Men walk by carrying rakes and scythes on their shoulders, women herd geese and cows. The light on this June afternoon is incandescent, making a *chiaroscuro* of the lupins, poppies, and wild roses that grow with abandon by the side of the road.

Olena, in flowered kerchief, tunic, and long skirt, stands beside her house. She is expecting us. As Cousin Roxolana and I emerge from our taxi, Olena holds out her wide, capable arms. I burst into tears as she kisses me three times, cheek and cheek and cheek again. *"Ridne, ridne, ridne,"* she repeats, which, roughly translated, means: original belonging, pertaining to roots. *Mine.*

I have been travelling through Ukraine for two weeks. After my time in Kyiv with Roxolana, I've struck out on my own, a girl with a camera and a rolling suitcase, an unusual sight in a country with no tourism to speak of. People stop me and ask me: *Why are you here?* Through the dirty windows of ancient buses, crowded trains, and ramshackle taxis, history reveals itself to me in one great fireball of memory and dishonesty. The green steppes that my father used to sing to us about are full of either half-built, gaping monster homes, or peasants in dire poverty. The old Babas, the heart and centre of our culture, have been abandoned, and are left to begging in the subways of bombed-out cities. Everyone I meet has an open wound they want to tell me about: a tragic death, murdered kin, or a slow graceless decline into poverty.

But now it's clear that all roads both taken and not originate here, in the *selo*, in the village of Schvaikivtsi, where my great aunt Olena, Baba's sister, greets me for the first time as tenderly as though I were her own daughter. Olena ushers us into her tiny house, and back in time one hundred years. I feel like I am walking onto a stage set. Dusty sepia photos of scowling family patriarchs hang crookedly on a wall. There are two overstuffed beds against either side of the whitewashed room, and in the middle, as though beneath a proscenium, a wooden table covered with newspapers. Actors in a family drama, Roxolana and I place our modest offerings there: a bouquet of roses; bananas and cherries from the market; a loaf of heavy rye bread. But the only thing Olena, more-or-less toothless, will eat is boiled eggs, which she serves without apology. In every gesture and glance of hers there is a feeling of certainty, of things occurring exactly as they should. I feel as though I should be here but also, strangely, as though I always have.

We only spend two hours with Olena, and it's odd how the time slows down, becomes almost still. It is warm in Olena's tiny house, but I am chilled by the uncanny sense of returning to the past, the dead and the living all present in this moment. We eat eggs, I pass around photographs. We talk about my grandmother, Olena's sister, who died two years earlier. Olena asks timid, halting questions about her sibling, who left for a better life, *za hranetsiu*, beyond the border, so very long ago. *Was she ill? Was she happy?*

The taxi driver stands outside, smoking, looking at his watch. Shockingly, it's time to leave.

Eggs were never a fancy dish in my family. If we had eggs, they were soft-boiled, and served in egg cups, buttered rye toast on the side. In Savella Stechishin's *Traditional Ukrainian Cookery*, there are only eight rather plain egg recipes (with the exception of the hilariously over-the-top "Stuffed Eggs with Mushroom Caps"), and they come with a severe admonition: "Ukrainians do not serve eggs with toast. In fact, toasted bread slices are practically unknown to them. Many Ukrainian newcomers to Canada find it difficult to become accustomed to toasted bread."

My favourite egg recipe is Spanish tortilla, which Lesya taught us all to make when she returned from a year of studying in Spain. Fry a sliced Spanish onion and two or three peeled, thinly sliced Russet potatoes in a good quantity of olive oil in a non-stick skillet until potatoes are tender, about twenty minutes. Remove the potatoes, leaving about one teaspoon of oil in the skillet (disposing of the rest). Mix the fried potatoes with a half-dozen beaten eggs. Heat up the skillet again, pour in the egg-potato mixture, cover with a lid, and cook on a low heat, loosening the bottom with a spatula every so often, until it sets around the edges, about ten to twelve minutes. The tricky part comes here. Slide the tortilla onto a large flat plate. Invert the skillet over the plate, and flip, so that the top of the tortilla is now on the bottom of the skillet. Cook, covered, for ten minutes more, then slide the tortilla, for a final time, onto the plate. You should have a lovely, light cake, which can be eaten hot or cold with a crisp green salad, crusty bread, and, if it's late enough in the day, a rough Spanish *rioja*.

Scrambled eggs and toast are what I eat when I have a cold or when I'm heartsick. More elaborate eggs mark the weekend: *chilaquiles* (corn tortilla strips sautéed with mild green chilies, cheese, and eggs) at Rhizome, a queer-run café on Broadway in Vancouver. These eggs have a spicy provenance: a recipe passed on to Lisa, one of the co-owners, from Socorro, a comrade in San Francisco, who got it from her family in Mexico.

There is the Mediterranean frittata I make only on Sundays, pungent with tomato, olives, basil, onions, and feta cheese. I eat it alone while reading the paper, listening to opera on the radio. I'm sometimes bemused by the solitary routines of my own life, thousands of miles from Olena's village, cultures and families disconnected by migration, linked for a moment by a smell, a certain quality of light, the texture and taste of eggs.

I go back to the village the next day, this time without Roxolana, which means that I must negotiate the festering crowd of taxi drivers on my own. They stand by their cars, smoking and gossiping in the middle of a dusty square. Did I imagine it, or did a deadly silence fall upon them as I approached? Did one of them stride over to me like a gunslinger, and was that why I ended up choosing the most psychotic driver of them all?

We depart in a toxic mushroom-cloud of exhaust, lurching onto the highway and then, just as suddenly, lurching off. "Excuse me, sir, but this doesn't look at all like the same road we took yesterday," I manage to say in Ukrainian. "For example, yesterday we drove on asphalt and here you are driving through a field."

"Asphalt?" shouts the driver, as though I'd just suggested that he drive through someone's house. "*Asphalt?*" he says again, his voice rising even louder in wild indignation. "Asphalt is for *cowards!*" At that, we fly over a rut in the cattle path that is serving as our highway, and I am tossed back against the seat. I huddle there, considering my options, which doesn't take long, since there are none. I have handed over my fate, and the equivalent of five dollars, to a madman. Houses and cattle fields I've never seen before are flying by; geese, cows, and children flee from our path with great urgency. I distract myself by wondering how long it will take to find my body, what kind of a funeral my relatives will throw together out here in the old country, what food will be served, and who will come.

Suddenly, we are on an actual road again, hurtling through what looks to be a village. An old woman looking very much like Aunt Olena walks by. "Stop!" I shout at the driver, and we screech to a sudden halt. By sheer dumb luck, we are in Schvaikivtsi. My great aunt stares impassively at us as I scold the driver for his recklessness. He offers to wait for me and, for an additional fee, drive me back to town, excellent bargain. I strongly discourage this and bid him goodbye. He grins blissfully and flies off in a steam of dust. Aunt Olena, still frozen in place, says only, "Nu, you recognized me."

The minute we get to her house, she cooks me some soft-boiled eggs. Instead of toast, a triumphant shot of amber-coloured vodka, redolent of herbs, accompanies the fresh, bright yellow yolks. It is ten in the morning.

We spend the rest of that lazy June day sitting out of doors. We talk, sing, or sit amicably in silence. Olena perches herself regally on the stoop of her house, sun gilding the beautiful network of wrinkles on her face. Children float around her like flies, and she periodically shoos them away. Villagers drift in and out of the yard. Everyone knows that "a guest from Canada" is visiting, but really, Olena is the main attraction. There is, for all of us, some comfort to be found in Olena's slow, measured way of talking, and in the continuity that her ninety-three years in this village provide.

Like most people of advanced age, Olena lives in the moment. The past is far too unwieldy; the future doesn't exist. I try to get her to talk about the two world wars she's lived through. Wearily, she tries to oblige me and then says, "I don't want to remember any more." Mostly, she talks about the small details of her life: the ache in her legs, the fur-lined boots she's wearing and how comfortable they are, the strawberries and new potatoes that are almost ready for harvest. Occasionally, she utters cryptic pronouncements in Ukrainian, which I attempt to translate in my head. "You must live in truth," she says mysteriously, her eyes squinting into the middle-distance of the horizon. "Live in truth, truthfully."

People are coming in from the fields on ox-drawn carts. The sun begins to slant gold across the fields. Geese and cows wander in from pasture. Cousin Roxolana, always several steps ahead of me, has arranged for a family friend to pick me up and drive me to the train station. Olena kisses me goodbye with a matter-of-fact sadness, and hands me a blue plastic bag of freshly laid eggs. She stands in the road watching us leave, a matrushka doll getting smaller and smaller until it disappears.

POTATOES

Anh told me that she and her sisters and her mother were always craving the food from home. They had arrived here as Chinese refugees, escaping persecution in Vietnam. They were one of the so-called "boat people" who came to Canada in great numbers in the 1970s. The Huas would walk along Spadina Avenue in Toronto, looking forlornly in all the windows of the Chinese and Vietnamese restaurants, wishing they were home. When they finally returned to Vietnam for a visit, they ate and ate: grilled chicken with lemongrass, pork kebabs, stuffed pancakes, pho. It made them sick. It tasted funny: not how they remembered.

Sometimes when I am lying in bed, reaching unsuccessfully for sleep, I think about food. I create a theme, like potatoes. In my head, I conjure up the different potato dishes my mother cooked when I was a child, and they fly magically across my mind's eye like a scene from *Bewitched*. New potatoes in cream and dill; potato pancakes; pork chops with scalloped potatoes. The backdrop for these reveries is always summer: there is a yellow and red swing set that clangs to a stop as Mama calls our names for dinner, and screen doors that slam open and shut all along the lane, *thwack, thwack, thwack*. Crickets and the sound of kids playing through the open window as we eat: meatloaf and mashed potatoes; homemade cinnamon buns for dessert. We swallow our food as quickly as we can, without being too obvious about it. The long prairie summer twilight calls out to us. There are so many things to do, like complex versions of hide and seek or Mother May I, or just sitting in the back alley and making plans for the next day as the lavender coolness of night slowly descends and the moms start calling the children home.

I now wonder if my mom enjoyed making those meals, recipes remembered from the old country, passed on from my grandmother or copied from friends. Once I snooped through my mother's tattered old recipe journal, imprinted with food stains from hundreds of meals. I was thrilled to find a recipe for "Sally's Potatoes," a time-saving classic from the 1950s, written in my mother's tiny, neat script: *Cook and mash potatoes. Add sautéed onion in butter, salt and pepper, milk and 1 egg. Form it into a shape and roll in crushed cornflakes. Put in oven and heat through.*

I wonder what changed for my mother as we—and she—got older, and potatoes took the form of frozen McCain's french fries, accompanying Swanson's turkey pot pies. We loved those meals too, eaten in front of the pale blue light of the television, and we still had our mashed potatoes with turkey or pot roast to look forward to on Sundays. By then my mother would have turned forty, as I did not too long ago. Turning forty, you see the expanse of your life for the first time, like getting onto a rise of land after driving through prairie for a very long while: where you came from, where you need to go. It hurts, to turn forty. Mama went back to school at age forty and so, come to think of it, did I. She used to say that getting her Bachelor's degree in French literature was more important to her than getting married and I puzzled over that then, but of course I don't, now.

I met Anh while completing my Master's degree in Toronto at the turn of the twenty-first century. We were taking the same class, a seminar on theories of sexuality. I found her beautiful, with her shoulder-length black hair and a ready, dazzling smile. She was giggly, and deeply intelligent. She was shy too, so it took some time, but finally, we become friends. On days when we'd had enough of books and academic bureaucracy, Anh and I would head to Chinatown for lunch. We'd walk along the wide avenue of Spadina, nudging each other when we saw a particularly beautiful or exotic vegetable amid the mountains of bok choy, coriander, bean sprouts, long green beans, small Thai eggplants, and watercress. We'd talk about food, and death, and diaspora, but even so we'd laugh a lot.

One day, Anh took me to her favourite Vietnamese restaurant where she graciously interpreted the menu for me. I told her about when my mother got involved in helping Vietnamese refugees in Ottawa, and suddenly everything she cooked was Asian: spring rolls, stir fries, grilled whole fish, not a potato in sight. I grew to love the clean, fresh taste of Vietnamese food. Food writer Madhur Jaffrey waxes eloquent about this cuisine: "Eating a morsel of Vietnamese food is often like strolling through a tropical garden and then, when the moment is right, taking a bite from it."

Anh and I ate salad rolls with peanut sauce, ground prawn wrapped around sugarcane, and barbecued chicken redolent of lemongrass and lime. I followed her lead as she ordered a tall cool drink with coconut milk in it. We talked for hours, then emerged back onto the steamy street and back north up Spadina, ending with a glass of wine on a terrace, ideas and theories building up between us like storm clouds.

After I returned to Vancouver, Anh came to visit me. I took her to a Ukrainian festival at the Plaza of Nations. There were Easter Egg demonstrations, displays of embroidery, dance performances. I made too many jokes, and hid behind my video camera. Through the camera lens, I thought I saw a kind of sadness in the eyes of the elderly there, and a hunger in their faces.

We lined up for Ukrainian food dispensed by female volunteers in embroidered blouses. Anh ordered exactly what I ordered: the perogy special. I asked her what she thought, and she described the feel in her mouth: *soft, sensual, luxurious*. I had never heard sexy words like that used for such an ordinary thing like mashed potatoes and cheese stuffed inside dough, a dish as old as my great aunt's memory, and even older still.

Dionne Brand writes, in *A Map to the Door of No Return*, "Too much has been made of origins." Some days you eat and eat and it just doesn't feel like home. Roots can nourish, but they can also develop a bitter taste. Sometimes, they can make you ill. That day, at the Plaza of Nations, I ached for something to feel familiar, but none of it did, not even the food.

FOOD FOR THE SOUL

There is a Ukrainian Christmas Eve tradition that hardly anyone observes anymore: laying an extra place setting for the dead. At Easter, again with the morbid customs: going out to the cemetery to bless the graves of your loved ones and then having a picnic lunch amid the tombstones. The idea being, of course, that the ghosts of the dead are always with us, the border between this life and the next permeable as a cloud.

My family is full of ghosts. They hide in the bookshelves, lurk in family snapshots, sing to music behind our backs. Our rituals of cooking and eating are a kind of memory machine, unleashing smells and tastes that evoke spectral presences.

Mikhailo was my father's brother. We were told he was an artist, and that he published cartoons that criticized the Bolsheviks. According to family apocrypha, Mikhailo was eventually arrested for his radical ways, killed, and buried in a mass grave. How do you remember an uncle you never met? Was he funny, was he a bit of a show-off, would he have made cartoons for us? In the liquor cabinet beside the whiskey, I can hear the conspiratorial chuckle of my grandfather (Dido), also named Mikhailo. Dido read to me from the Saturday funnies, made me ham sandwiches on weekends, and often had liquor on his breath. Downtown Vancouver continues to be haunted by the ghost-music of my brother Roman, his delicate cadences embroidering the air. Great Aunt Olena lives in my head, with her pithy expressions and sense of history, and Baba, she's always in the kitchen, wafting around us in the smell of cabbage rolls and borscht and her eternal melancholy. We made peace with these ghosts early on; we had to. We wanted them in our lives.

There are other ghosts as well: the ghosts of those who die in every war, with their sad laughter, their unheeded admonitions. And the niggling, uncomfortable ghosts of those still alive: lost lovers, or friends who have drifted away.

French philosopher Jacques Derrida had a great respect for ghosts. Not quite alive and yet not quite dead, they seemed to him to be a perfect example of the dissolution of binaries, a challenge to either/or. He felt that those who had gone before could teach us how to live. A ghost is an archive, a resource. Derrida suggested that we learn to live with ghosts, "in the upkeep, the conversation, the company, or the companionship, in the commerce without commerce of ghosts. To live otherwise, and better."

In my family, it's not necessary to lay a place setting for the dead. They're always with us, encouraging us to eat, and love, and live better.

THANKSGIVING DINNER

It had been a season of rain, of a bruised, bluish-grey sky, of watery green landscapes. The dash and slash of yellow leaves punctuated the urban scenery, pressed against pavement or left dangling, like ornaments, from the dark wet branches of trees. Headlines in news boxes flashed at us like so many black and white film frames: *America Under Attack*. *America At War*. It was just after 9/11: a season in which we longed to turn to one another—for information, for comfort, for company. Everything had changed, we were told. We needed to find our own epistemology, ways of knowing that were still there, bedrock beneath the turmoil of world affairs.

And so I invited six women for Thanksgiving dinner. It was a welcome-home party of sorts for Penny, who had been in Toronto far too long. But it was also an excuse to create a feast, to luxuriate in the flicker of candles, the warmth of good conversation and decent wine. I kept the menu relatively simple: roast turkey with apricot stuffing, Brussels sprouts, mashed potatoes, my mother's mushroom sauce. Penny would make *tsimmes*, Haida would bring salad, Megan the pumpkin pie. I was well-organized, or so I thought. I went to the Granville Island Public Market the day before, picking up an organic turkey and perusing the glistening pyramids of vegetables. After purchasing everything I needed, I bought a cup of coffee and an apple-cardamom Danish and sat outside, facing the harbour, smelling the sea. It felt good to do something as ordinary as enjoying a pastry while savouring a view. Everywhere I'd been that month—the university, the street, the Main Street bus—there was fear in the air.

I made the stuffing early the next morning: sourdough bread, minced dried apricots, sunflower seeds, garlic, and thyme. Penny came over later in the day to make the *tsimmes*, that traditional Jewish dish with its extraordinary juxtaposition of different sweetnesses: yams, apples, and prunes. While she did that, I prepped the mushrooms and fresh dill for the sauce, then stuffed the turkey, brushing it with olive oil and lemon, dusting generously with paprika. I mentally calculated the cooking time: by putting it in the oven now, I estimated we'd be eating by seven.

Everyone arrived at six, just as the poignant aromas of roasting meat and vegetables were making themselves known. I lit candles, poured glasses of wine. Rita laid out the hors d'oeuvres she'd brought: crostini, hummus, antipasto spread. We were a group of women who didn't usually get together, but we fell into conversation with relief. A raucous humour spread through the room as we talked. I moved back and forth between kitchen and living room, putting the potatoes on, stirring the sauce. I was flushed with the heat of the stove and with the pleasure of a house full of people, a kitchen in benevolent culinary chaos.

At 6:45, I checked the turkey. I pulled it out, smelled it, touched it. In truth, I had never roasted a turkey before, but I had watched my mother do it often enough. This one seemed pallid and flaccid, somehow. I called Cynthia over: I figured that, having raised a child, and, presumably, having roasted many turkeys, she could advise me. She tweaked the legs and declared that they weren't loose enough. Haida, also a mother, was summoned. She poked the skin with a fork and we watched silently as the telltale pink liquid trickle leaked out.

Cynthia sighed wearily. It was quite obvious that we would not be eating for some time.

I returned the turkey to the oven, turned off the flame beneath the pot of potatoes. Rita, an ex-affair, got all flirtatious as she usually did in times of crisis, and poured me another glass of Merlot. At that very moment, habitually-late Megan arrived, laden with pies and her usual flurry of apologies (which is why we always assign the dessert to her). She seemed chastened to find out that she had, in fact, arrived well in advance of dinner.

We settled in. Rita, attentive to a fault, fed me a crostini and gave me a quick, sexy shoulder-massage. I passed around more hors d'oeuvres, made sure everyone's glass was full, put on another CD. Then we did what everyone had been doing lately: we recalled where we'd been on September 11, or what we'd been doing. Penny had been at an anti-poverty meeting in Toronto, lucky enough to be in the company of other activists like herself. Conversation had been critical, wary of a new world order. Rita had been at home; she said, "I immediately went out onto the street. I needed to see other people." I admitted that my life as a writer was so damnably isolated, I hadn't heard the news until late in the morning and then, dissociating, had gone underwear shopping—for hours. While others talked about shedding tears that day, I had gone numb, and didn't cry until, days later, I watched a Muslim child say to a TV camera: "I will try to look innocent."

I talked about the bus I take, to and from work, where war is ongoing: a driver bullies a man who doesn't have a ticket (even after someone else pays his fare); frail bodies weaving and huddling along the sidewalk at the corner of Hastings and Main, the heart of Vancouver's impoverished Downtown Eastside. The war at home: the money that will somehow be found for missiles, stolen from the poor.

Someone got up to check the turkey, I changed the CDs yet again. Hugh Marsh playing "Amazing Grace" on violin; Cassandra Wilson singing "Sankofa." We talked about our fears. As long-time social activists, we were seeing forty years of feminist and anti-racist work crumble before our eyes. Increased border surveillance and racial profiling; no skepticism, let alone dissent; everybody channelling CNN. I described the deep talking that had taken place in my classroom: a South Asian woman who shared a story of her son being harassed on a bus; a Persian woman who told the harrowing tale of being taken in for questioning at the airport, and kept there for hours.

The smell of roasted turkey and garlic filled the room, but for a time, we forgot about dinner. We talked until eleven at which point the turkey was pronounced officially cooked. Roasted garlic was mashed into the potatoes, salad was tossed. We crowded around my ridiculously small kitchen table, and together we ate the turkey along with the stuffing, the *tsimmes*, Cynthia's rhubarb chutney, and Kim's homemade cranberry sauce. We all had seconds, groaning about how delicious the food was. We returned to the living room for pie and coffee. Arms and legs grew languid, people stretched out on the sofa and onto pillows on the floor. It was well after one a.m. when I bid my last guest goodbye.

In the days and weeks that followed, we ran into one another other at various demonstrations and meetings and candlelight vigils. The sky by then was a daily smudge of grey, the mountains a faint blue watercolour wash behind them. The new anti-terrorist bill and Canada's pledging of troops to aid in the bombing of Afghanistan were keeping us busy; our email inboxes overflowed with announcements, petitions, and protests. Rita said, "It was so good just to *talk*"; Penny commented, in her wry way, that I really should undercook a turkey more often.

TSIMMES

This recipe is from The Moosewood Cookbook, *by Molly Katzen.*

LIST 1:
2 lbs yams, peeled
2 large carrots
1 large apple, peeled
1 onion
20 large, pitted prunes
Juice of 1 lemon
1 tsp salt
½ tsp cinnamon
⅔ cup fresh-squeezed orange juice

LIST 2:
2 eggs, beaten
¼ cup breadcrumbs
½ tsp salt
3 tbsp cold butter, thinly sliced

Preheat the oven to 350° F. Grate half the yams and set aside. Cut the rest of the yams into bite-sized chunks. Mix List 1 ingredients together, except for the reserved, grated yams, and place mixture in a buttered deep-dish casserole. In a bowl, mix List 2 together, except the butter. Add the grated yams to this mixture, and then place over first mixture in casserole. Dot with the sliced butter. Cover tightly with casserole lid or aluminum foil and bake for 1 hour, then remove cover and bake for another hour. Tsimmes should be lightly browned when done. Can be eaten as a main dish meal, with salad, or as an accompaniment to roast chicken or turkey. Makes 6 servings.

VEGETABLE CURRY

I'd be on a bus on Granville Street and hear my brother's music through the open window, in counterpoint to the whoosh of the bus doors and the mutter of traffic. I'd steel myself against his silken melodies floating in the air, then allow myself a quick glance, to make sure he was OK. If he saw me, he'd scowl and look away. The bus would continue on its way and my brother would move past me like a short scene in a film.

The rest of my family lived in other parts of Canada. Whenever they were in Vancouver, the first thing they'd say was, "Let's go find Roman." I'd be reluctant, because it was way too easy for *me* to find him. Sometimes I'd say, "He doesn't want to be found." I was right and I was wrong, and I knew it.

On a March day full of blowsy cherry blossoms and gusting white clouds, my niece Sonya came to visit me during spring break. Sure enough, as soon as she got to my house, she said, "Let's go find Roman." There was a strange glitter in her eyes and an urgency to her voice that made me listen. Sonya was only sixteen, but already her life was complex and full of trouble. We took the bus to Granville Street, and followed the sound of Roman's music. I brought along my lover Krys for extra support, and I had a back-up event for us planned in case Roman was in a bad mood. But there he was, in a sharp second-hand tweed coat, a crisp shirt, and dress pants, like he knew company was coming. Roman was a moody, cantankerous guy, and he'd been nasty to me more times than he'd been genial. But he could see his niece standing in front of him so innocently, like a fresh sheet in the wind, that spring afternoon. He smiled shyly and played a song just for her. Krys pulled out a camera and Roman politely posed for photographs so I could send them to my mom, so she could see he was OK. *Snap:* Roman with his bandura like a shield in front of him, smiling sweetly; Sonya looking up at him, face illuminated. Me a little further away, a taut, nervous smile on my face; Krys's tall, protective shadow in the corner of the frame.

To my surprise, Roman offered to meet us in a café in an hour, after he'd finished playing for the day. I didn't expect to see him again that afternoon or that week, but he did show up, a half-hour late, as we finished our coffee. His pockets were bulging with small apologetic gifts he'd bought from the hippie street vendors along the way. He gave me some prayer beads. I felt embarrassed, thrown off. He was stirring his coffee with shaky hands and asking Sonya questions about her life. She was looking happy for the first time since she'd arrived. Krys was watching the whole weird scene like it was *Days of Our Lives.* I was curious to see what else could possibly happen. I invited Roman to join Sonya, Krys, and me for dinner.

Vegetable curry is a dish I used to make a lot. It is hippie-ish comfort food, a variation on stirfry, really. It bears little or no relation to any of the multi-layered tastes and textures of the curries you can get at Delhi Darbar or Rubina Tandoor, Indian restaurants in Vancouver. My vegetable curry has a Thai inflection, only because those were the ingredients easily available at my local greengrocer. It's easy, flexible, cheap, and kind of boring, like comfort food should be.

As soon as we got home, I put basmati rice on the boil and set to work sautéeing onions and garlic, chopping potatoes, peppers, and carrots. Krys hid behind the newspaper, nervously crossing and uncrossing her long legs. Sonya and

Roman sat at the kitchen table and talked: about what Vancouver was like to live in, about what the other nieces were up to, about memories from dysfunctional family Christmases past. Once the onions and garlic had become soft and translucent, I threw in the chopped vegetables and a little bit of water, so they could steam. The kitchen window clouded up. Roman was telling a funny story from when we were kids, and Sonya, chin in hand, was giggling hesitantly, unsure of how long anything would last.

I added some Mae Ploy red curry paste mixed with coconut milk and some fresh-squeezed lime juice into the vegetable mix, as well as some vegetable stock, and a dash of Asian fish sauce, too. I let the mixture simmer for twenty minutes or so while I pulled out dishes and cutlery. Krys chopped cilantro to put on the table, along with a big bowl of yogurt. I liked seeing her graceful hands manipulate the knife; I enjoyed the feeling of her solid, stocky body near me, in the same room as my brother and my niece.

As I served up the steaming bowls of curry, I watched Roman out of the corner of my eye. I figured he was more used to fare from Wendy's and McDonald's. But he ate ravenously, quickly, finishing off the bowl of curry and rice in four minutes flat, and then shyly asking for more. "I never knew vegetables could be so tasty," he said, with a kind of wonder in his voice. Krys shot me a look of concern, thinking he was joking—with my family, you could never tell. But in that moment, I wanted him to come over for Sunday dinner every single week, knit him a sweater with a snowflake pattern on it, make him soup from scratch. I guess what I was feeling was love, though I didn't realize it at the time.

After dinner, Krys slipped away, grimacing dramatically as she closed the door. I pulled out my absurd Travel Scrabble, with its portable board that was not much bigger than a handkerchief. My brother's big fingers handled the letters clumsily, like tiny bombs, as words like T-R-A-G-I-C and S-H-A-B-B-Y formed across the board. Sonya was in hyper teenage mode, drifting in and out of the room, calling friends, checking email, messaging her sisters Natalie and Chrissy. My brother and I started talking about my dad, who had died the year before, and we awkwardly traded stories, told in the same minor key.

"Did I ever tell you about the time I sent him a letter in Ukrainian?" I said. (For some reason we always said *him*, never *Tato*, or Dad.) "He, like, sent it back to me covered in red ink!"

"Uh, red ink?" said Roman, shifting uncomfortably in his chair. He could see I was about to go into a rant. He'd never really enjoyed my rants.

"Yeah! He corrected the whole letter, like it was one of his damn students' essays!"

"Wow," said Roman, looking around to make sure he remembered where the exit was, and then fingering the mickey of vodka I knew was in his coat pocket. I was dying for a drink, too, but I thought I had to stay sober, set an example.

"He said you used to write to him." I was unwilling to let go of this topic.

"Uh, yeah. He lent me money to make a CD. We were on a payment plan. So once a month I'd send him a cheque and a letter."

"Did he write back?"

"Oh yeah. He loved to criticize my drinking and my busking. But, whatever. At least we were in touch. We wrote letters back and forth to each other for a couple of years. It was OK." Roman took a gulp of tea and then sat back and crossed his arms self-protectively around his chest, staring down at the table.

We kept talking. Roman told me he'd gone briefly into detox, but that it hadn't taken, except that he now admitted he was an alcoholic. The beer halls on Hastings Street were his living room, and the people in it were interesting, fragile, smart—his community. Then, out of the blue, he said, "I'm not someone who has much physical touch in my life, so when someone hugs me I remember the smell. I remember Baba smelled like soap." It was a moment of unexpected intimacy, a warm wind on a cold day, and it upset me in some ineffable way.

The evening waned to a close. Roman offered to take a day off busking and show Sonya around. That tour was to be the last time she saw him, though of course none of us knew that then. That night, I couldn't sleep, and the words we'd exchanged tumbled uneasily, a jangle of precious coins, through my mind.

Sonya had a strange, wonderful time with Roman the next day. She told me that he took her to a nice Italian restaurant on Lonsdale Quay for lunch, and then for a walk through the Downtown Eastside. "He walked through it all with such a stride," she said proudly. "And he told me all these statistics, like how many people go to this soup kitchen every day or how many people live in that shelter. I felt like he was showing me his home. But, like, in a way where he didn't want to take away my innocence, either." Her small, honest face glowed as she told me this.

My brother turned his head away from me the next time I saw him on Granville Street. I persisted, and uttered a weak hello; he snarled a response and kept playing his music. I walked away. There seemed to be no residue of that warm evening in my kitchen on a chilly spring night, the windows fogged up, the sweet and sour aroma of basmati, onions, lime, and curry emanating from the stove.

After that, we started to avoid each other more pointedly, and then we got used to it, the way you get used to west coast rain, or the distant lament of the foghorn in winter. It's never comfortable, but it starts to be part of you.

These days, a thin cloud of regret and remorse hangs over me whenever I think about my brother. *I'm not someone who has much physical touch in my life.* Did I even think to hug him when I said goodbye? Why didn't I try harder, extend those Sunday dinner invitations, give him stuff, place a care-fully-folded sweater beside his busking spot and walk away? Why weren't there more evenings to remember? Sometimes I wonder if we were just plain scared of each other, my brother and I—of how we were so alike, in so many ways.

That evening of vegetable curry and Scrabble is one thing I have, something *he* gave to *me*, though of course he didn't know it then.

LOST AND FOUND

Everything slowed down, that one hot week in July: not slow-motion, like in a schmaltzy romantic film, but rather a series of spare, isolated scenes, black leader in between. Food punctuated those moments, gave structure to chaos, something to hold onto for the length of a meal.

My sister Lydia called me with the news. My brother Roman's body had been found in his hotel room. Dead from a heart attack, age forty-two. I had just come back from a hike on the North Shore. The day, brilliantly sunny, closed down immediately, like the shutter of a camera. I called Megan: she came over right away. She knew her job was to remain stoic and calm while I wept, but I thought I detected her wiping away a tear after I got off the phone to my brother Michael. Everyone in Vancouver knew Roman. He was part of the urban landscape we called home.

My youngest brother showed up at my door the next day. Michael, the jovial world traveller, the handsome guy you could never quite pin down, looked at me with tired, pale blue eyes, an unbearable sadness there. We embraced gingerly, like each of us were made of glass. Then we set to work, completing a list of awful tasks: to recover my brother's body from the city morgue; to gather Roman's personal effects; to organize a funeral.

My brother and I sat stiffly across from each other in my small living room, a coffee table between us, a lit candle upon it. We hardly glanced at each other as we made to-do lists and took turns making difficult phone calls. If we had looked, we'd have noticed that my brother, now a ghost, was no longer between us.

Losing a sibling shifts your position in the birth order. Roman, younger than me, older than Michael, had always provided a bulwark between us. As troubled and moody as he was, I'd always identified more with Roman, my fellow artist, my fellow outcast. I never related to Michael's sleek presentation, his suits, his distant, worldly ways, so much like *Tato*. But suddenly we were five siblings, not six. I felt closer than ever to my youngest brother, at the same time that I realized I hardly knew him at all.

I put some of Roman's music on the CD player; we made more calls: to a taciturn, suspicious city coroner; to a funeral director; to my tearful, confused mother. I wasn't hungry, but out of a habit of hospitality I served Michael a simple lunch: a roasted potato salad I'd made the day before. "Wow. That tastes really good," said Michael earnestly as he gulped it down. He sounded just like Roman.

During the course of our terse conversation and awkward silences, I learned some things that day. Like how close Michael felt to Roman, only sixteen months between them. He told me about the fights they used to have as kids, protracted wrestling matches that Roman always won. I saw how protective Michael was, too. He told me that whenever he was in Vancouver, he'd track Roman down and give him new clothes, and then they'd go drinking together on skid row.

Michael and I drove to the police station to retrieve Roman's sole valuable possession. In the lost and found department, a clerk sat behind a cage reading a paperback, shelves and shelves of seized items behind him. He shuffled away sullenly to get what we'd come for. When the man emerged with Roman's bandura, Michael gasped involuntarily. He took Roman's beloved instrument gently, reverently into his arms and, very slowly, carried it to the car. "I feel like I'm carrying his body," was all he said.

Michael and I retrieved the rest of Roman's few possessions from his room, stuffing them frantically into green garbage bags, to be sorted later: a sheaf of music; a boombox; a closetful of clothes; a collection of ceramic angels. An envelope of letters from my father. I found it hard to breathe; I was choking on air thick with my brother's presence: random particles of devotion, shame, anger, and love.

It was difficult to leave that room; it was impossible to stay. We went down into the lobby, where I called Penny. Michael said, "I'm going back up there for a minute to make a quick prayer."

Afterwards, we met up with Penny and Michael's girlfriend Ivanka in a downtown bar and drank an excessive amount of vodka, which seemed to have no effect. By then, Michael and I had spent six hours together, and that sweet intensity suddenly seemed painful. We parted ways until the next day. Penny and I went back to my house to make more phone calls and arrangements. I realized I hadn't eaten all day so, taking charge, Penny ordered takeout from Delhi Darbar, our usual favourites: butter chicken, vegetable jalfrezi, pulao rice, naan bread.

It was a warm, golden July evening, the sun just starting to set, the mountains blue and green against a lavender sky. But my body felt cold, chilled to the bone. As I cycled along 6th Avenue on my way to pick up the food, I saw Roman's hotel room in my mind's eye. This time it was pristine, completely empty, sheer curtains blowing in a breeze, awash with light.

I felt an unmistakable sense of relief. His, not mine.

TORTE

My mother came to visit me for seven days, a month after Roman died. I met her at the airport, unsure of how things would go.

Mama and I had never been close. We had traded more bitter words than kind, had made each other weep with frustration, and then spent years not calling or writing. Since Roman's death, we had both been making more of an effort. Still, there remained acrid moments between us, a sour taste after something good; you don't know why it's there. A babble of need and anger would pour from my throat when I was around my mother. I wanted her to accept me, all of me: my books, my lovers, my art. The imprecise limits of love—of hers and mine—made of me a harridan, cajoling, then wheedling, then criticizing.

In all the years I'd lived away from home, my mother never paid a visit longer than forty-eight hours. Those were rare, formal occasions, a benevolent monarch greeting her distant queer subject. But now, in the airport, what I saw was an elegant, determined lady in a red pantsuit, a colourful scarf around her neck. White hair set perfectly: she'd been to the hairdresser that very morning. She wanted things to go all right. Blue eyes, the exact same shade as my own, that I could barely look into, for fear I'd see my own feelings reflected there.

I was overly jolly and attentive as I hauled my mother's bags out the airport's sliding doors and into the crystalline light of a Pacific Northwest summer. During the cab ride home, I was a clownish tour guide, pointing out the sights: look, there are the mountains; over there, the leaky condominiums; on your left, a white guy in dreadlocks playing hacky sack. Suddenly, right there in the cab, Mama dug deeply and mysteriously into her carry-on bag and took out an inverted plastic Reddi-Wip tub. With a modest sense of drama, she pulled away the domed cover and there, on the upside-down Reddi-Wip lid, was a perfect, miniature shortcrust (*kruchei*) torte, my favourite dessert, and one which I had not eaten since childhood.

Savella Stechishin, author of the Ukrainian housewife's bible, *Traditional Ukrainian Cookery,* traces a popular history of torte that has its roots in early alliances and trade with European monarchies: "great banquets ... topped with a fabulous assortment of delightful pastries, marzipans, nougats and what-nots in fancy shapes...." This was an era of such reverence for torte that they were usually named after national and local heroes. But peasants baked them too, claims Stechishin, because even the poorest farmer had a cow and a chicken and perhaps even beehives, so that the essential ingredients of torte—butter, egg yolks, honey—were abundant. Stechishin takes us through the privations of the Soviet era, when elaborate desserts fell into disrepute as a marker of bourgeois decadence. But she notes happily that, in most Ukrainian cookbooks these days, there are more dessert and pastry recipes than any other category. She fondly describes how pastry recipes are handed from mother to daughter, but then ends her elegy to torte rather gloomily: "Unfortunately, [tortes] are far too rich for a Canadian generation of bathroomscale [sic] watchers. This book contains only a limited number of torte recipes that are adaptable to Canadian use." Nonetheless, she can't resist including a baker's dozen of torte recipes which, when combined, demand some six pounds of butter, over twenty-one cups of sugar, and ninety eggs.

Now, just to clarify things, Mama did not bake the torte she brought. Every Ukrainian cook has her specialty tortes, and this, I knew, was not one of my mom's. Her delicacies ran more towards a simple harmony of coffee and chocolate flavours, not the complex, polyphonic, almost crisp, almost tart-sweet richness of this concoction. Mama's friend Sonya (we called her Big Sonya, to distinguish her from my niece), who lives down the hall from her, remembered that I loved it, and sent it along, so practically packaged, with my mom.

It was a tender, thoughtful gesture. Roman had died just weeks earlier. I was only just beginning to understand my feelings. Sadness tumbled with guilt, relief, and shame, in a gritty, unsettling combination.

Weeks earlier, during the preparations for the funeral lunch in Edmonton, in Big Sonya's crammed, humid kitchen, I had blithely mentioned I was craving shortcrust torte. What I was really longing for, though, was comfort, and maternal solace, and what I wanted, at that very moment, was to curl up and fall asleep on Sonya's large, floury, apron-covered lap, to return to childhood, to a time when my brother was still a mischievous, scowling young boy, still alive. But there were cold cuts to arrange, Mama's mocha wafer torte to be sliced, a funeral to attend, a eulogy to deliver. I had to act like the big grown-up sister I needed to be: for my brother, for my mother, for myself. I immediately forgot my childlike demand, but here, weeks later, it had materialized.

My mother and I ate many things that week. For all of our bitterly argued differences, we have one big thing in common: an abiding fascination with the ways and meanings of the culinary arts. Food creates a kind of dialogue between us, an implicit assent missing in other aspects of each other's lives. We clip soup recipes from the newspaper; we plan improbable meals we will never cook. We read *Food and Wine*, and *Saveur*, and *Cook's Illustrated* like it's the smuttiest porn.

That week, I wanted to give my mother and myself a reprieve from the slow, hard labour of grieving. We ate and cooked with determination. When she arrived, I fed her freshly made gazpacho, which she ate with serious, silent approval; the next day, she fed me her homemade potato-cheese perogies with chicken stew, which I reverently devoured. I took Mama to restaurants and cafés I knew she'd like: to a place on the boardwalk in the fishing village of Steveston for clam chowder and crab cakes; to a café on Granville Island for chocolate ganache. My mother filled my freezer with perogies and borscht; months later, I was still finding the single-serving portions she had quietly tucked away for me.

And every evening, while sitting in front of the TV, we shared some kruchei torte and a cup of Earl Grey tea. The torte, my mother told me, takes about three days to make. There are the four or five shortcrust layers, which must be made first to flaky, delicate specifications. Then there are three different kinds of fillings—apple, apricot, and chocolate—and a thin white glaze that goes over everything. No doubt the fillings take time to set and cool, and assembly itself must be a tricky operation. My mother is somewhat dismissive whenever she talks about this torte. There is an implication of frivolity, perhaps even decadence. My mother, with six children to raise, had little time or patience for shortcrust pastry.

The torte lasted about as long as my mother's visit. I guarded it, and my mother, jealously. Only a select few of my friends were allowed to pay homage, and even fewer of these were offered torte.

My mother and I had a routine. Immediately after breakfast, my ma would start cooking: one day it was *lokshyna* (noodles with cabbage), another day, blueberry perogies. Then, we'd head into the city: to the Sun Yat-Sen Garden; over to Chinatown; up to Granville Street; back down Main. Our conversation was perfunctory, awkward: what ingredients to purchase for dinner; whether I needed a new frying pan, she'd seen a good one at The Bay. Those years of silence between us had deprived us of easy speech. In the late afternoon we'd head home, and Mama would lie down on the chaise lounge I had placed for her under the apple tree in my backyard. I'd sit in a lawn chair beside her and read, looking up every so often to watch the afternoon's dance of light and shadow pass over my mother's pale, drawn face.

We didn't talk very much about Roman. We didn't have to. He was there in every gesture, in the reason for my mother's visit, in the way I took care of her, in the way we had decided to let bygones be bygones. That week, I noticed a kind of lightness to my mother, like the grief had emptied her out somehow. I noticed how hard it was for me to be a daughter, to let my mother take care of me. I wished my brother could be there. I felt a bit guilty, like I was receiving a double-portion of my mother's love, like I was getting his share, too.

KRUCHEI TORTE (SHORTCRUST TORTE)

1 cup butter
¼ cup icing sugar
Juice and rind of 1 lemon
1 cup walnuts, ground
1 egg
2 cups all-purpose flour, sifted

Preheat oven to 350°F. In a bowl, cream butter and sugar. Add
the rest of the ingredients, ending with the flour. Mix well. Divide
dough into four parts. Cover with waxed paper and refrigerate for
at least 1 hour.

Butter two springform cake pans. Dip your hands in flour, then
pat one part of the dough into each cake pan. Bake in oven for
15–20 minutes, or until golden brown. Remove pan. Cool slightly,
then remove crusts and place on cake rack or clean dishtowels.
Butter pans again and bake the remaining two pieces of dough.

APPLE FILLING:
6 apples, peeled and cut into small thin pieces
Juice of 1 lemon
Pinch of cinnamon
Sugar to taste

In a pot on medium-high heat, cook all ingredients until apples are
soft—the consistency of applesauce—then cool.

APRICOT FILLING:
8 oz dried apricots
1 tsp sugar or apricot jam

In a pot on medium-high heat, cook apricots until soft. Strain, then purée in a blender or food processor. Add sugar or jam. Reheat until sweetener dissolves.

CHOCOLATE FILLING:
6 tbsp butter
10 tbsp icing sugar, sifted
1 egg
2 tbsp cocoa

In a bowl, cream butter and sugar. Add egg and cocoa and mix until smooth.

Spread each shortcrust layer with a different filling: use the apple filling on the first layer and the chocolate filling on the second layer. Spread the third layer with the apricot filling. Cover with the fourth shortcrust layer.

WHITE GLAZE:
2 cups powdered sugar
approx. ¼ cup whipping cream
1½ tsp vanilla or almond extract

In a bowl, combine sugar and vanilla. Whisk in whipping cream until desired texture is achieved (do not make it too thin, or it won't stick!).

Ice the top and sides of the assembled torte with the glaze. Let sit for 24 hours before serving.

MUSHROOMS

In my childhood there were always divas, common as borscht, thick as thieves. Women with bosoms you wanted to lay your head on, with earrings as big as dinner plates, hair piled high as the onion domes that made our church visible for miles along the flat prairie horizon. These were the ladies of the church, the pourers of tea, the makers of perogies and cabbage rolls, the first sopranos of the church choir. Defiant, bossy, and tragic, the Divas of the Church carried the weight of the diaspora on their shoulders. It fell to them the task of nagging their children to speak their mother tongues; of propping up their moody husbands traumatized by war; of wheedling cash for the churches that would save us all. These ladies, rarely silent, had mouths lined with lipsticks named Passion or Caprice; lips that formed the words of epithets, national anthems, and high-pitched hallelujahs.

My mother got sick the year after Roman died. This doubling of tragedy did not scare the Divas off, not one little bit. As soon as they heard that my mother had cancer of the larynx, they swung into action. They had all slowed down some, and their eyes showed the passing of the years, but they were as feisty and as powerful as ever. Their range of roles spanned far more than one octave; crisis was part of their repertoire.

I went to Edmonton to stay with my mother after she had surgery. Little Sonya picked me up at the airport and we drove straight to the hospital. Sonya had changed since I'd last seen her. There was a new softness and beauty to her, but a kind of world-weariness too, like she'd given up on some things, and discovered others. Since Roman's death she'd reconnected with my mother, and they seemed to enjoy their differences, arguing and reconciling, over and over again.

My mother burst into tears when I walked into her hospital room. Sonya sat down matter-of-factly on the bed beside my mother; she was comfortable there. I stood awkwardly, taking in the new knowledge of my mother's body and how surgery had changed it. I swallowed back salt water and guilt and unease, and decided then and there to give my ma what I hadn't been able to give my brother: to be someone she could lean on, no matter what. It was a peculiar equation; it didn't quite add up. But it made sense that afternoon, in the white cube of a hospital room.

When my mother got home, all she wanted to eat was mushrooms. It became an obsession. Sleepily adrift in clouds of crumpled Kleenexes and bottles of pills, she rose up off the couch and gathered all of her strength to make mushroom sauce. She wouldn't accept my help. With only one useable arm, she somehow managed to wash and chop a handful of mushrooms and sauté them in butter. Then, reserving the mushrooms, she browned some flour. In went as much cream as possible—she needed to gain back the weight she'd lost in hospital. She stirred and stirred while two potatoes, which had taken her twenty minutes to peel, boiled alongside.

And that was the easy part. When I came back into the kitchen, she'd been trying to get her food down for half an hour but had only managed to swallow two bitefuls. Courage, that long, fevered June in Edmonton, was defined by the image of my mother, a slight, dignified lady in her seventies, taking an hour and a half to eat two ounces of mashed potatoes and mushroom sauce.

After several days of this, I called one of the Divas and

asked her if she had any good mushroom recipes up her sleeve. She snorted with derision: the Divas were, of course, already on the case. With the precision and discipline of military commanders, they had phoned, they had conferred, they had prepped, and they had cooked. They went to the market, they defrosted Becel Margarine containers of chicken stock, they fried up *pitpenky*—dark, woody mushrooms they'd smuggled in from Ukraine, defying all manner of surveillance and terrorist threat. For the rest of the month, the Divas brought my mother mushroom soup in all its forms: big iron pots of mushroom-barley soup, tupperware containers of vegetable soup with mushroom broth, homemade cream of mushroom soup in a mason jar.

Did my mother and the other Divas know that mushrooms are known to have many immune-boosting properties? Egyptian Pharaohs hoarded mushrooms, forbidding them to commoners, while the Romans passed laws declaring mushrooms sacred and dubbing them "Food of the Gods." Mushrooms have been crucial to Chinese medicine for centuries, containing, as they do, vitamins B, C, and D. They are known to lower both blood pressure and serum cholesterol, and are considered by some to play a role in preventing cancer.

But that month, the Divas of the Church did more than make mushroom soup; they also took care of the mysterious, important details regarding my mother's recovery.

I was working behind the scenes, doing laundry, buying groceries, arranging for homecare, getting prescriptions filled. During those long, air-conditioned afternoons, I plunged like a snorkeller into colourful yet dangerous emotional shoals. There, a pure blue rage at the cancer industry, the pharmaceutical drugs my mother took each day, their pernicious after-effects; here, a flaccid, pale yellow sadness at mid-afternoon when I thought about my brother. Sadness not at his death anymore, but at my own inability to ever come to terms with it, to rise from it and surface, gulping clean, new air.

I lost myself in my mother's needs and the intimate demands of her body. I had to tie her shoes for her, change her dressings, rub cream into her arms and back. Some days, she wept on my shoulder. I began to imagine that my mother's survival depended only on me.

The Divas, scornful of my hubris, worked cleverly around me. They'd show up at my mother's condo when I least expected them, performing tasks I'd never asked them to do. One afternoon I came home, sweaty and disheveled from shopping and errand running, to find my mother dressed, sitting at the kitchen table, flanked by two of the Divas. They were doing her hair, pulling out hot rollers, brushing out curls. The kitchen I'd scrupulously cleaned just that morning was strewn with hair products, damp towels, combs, and hair clips. I said hello, but everyone ignored me. The air was full of sly gossip and laughter. Tea and chocolate marble bundt cake had been served (I could see the crumbs), and none had been saved for me.

No matter: my mother was smiling for the first time in weeks, flushed with the pleasure of attention. Her hair was shining, curled, and combed. I think she was wearing lipstick, too. Another vat of mushroom soup stood cooling on the counter, offering a woodsy aroma.

I left the room and went to call a travel agent to book a ticket home.

MUSHROOM SAUCE

This recipe is adapted from Savella Stechishin's Traditional Ukrainian Cookery.

3 tbsp butter
1 cup mushrooms, chopped
2 tbsp flour
½ cup chicken stock
½ cup thin cream
½ tsp salt
2 tbsp fresh dill, chopped
Pepper to taste

In a saucepan on medium-high heat, melt 1 tablespoon of the butter and sauté mushrooms for a few minutes, until soft. Remove mushrooms and reserve. Add remaining butter to pan, melt it, and blend in the flour. Add stock, cream, and salt. Stir slowly but steadily over direct heat until sauce comes to a boil. Cook over low heat for about 5 minutes, or until sauce is thickened. Add mushrooms, dill, and pepper to taste. Makes 4 servings.

CHICKEN

I ran into Jacky, my upstairs neighbour, as I got off the Broadway bus. She was on her way to Kingsgate, an aging, dimly lit mall full of dollar stores and ladies with clipboards taking surveys—the Faustian site of horror and regret we routinely referred to as "Hellsgate." We stood on the corner for a while, catching up on local gossip, talking over the roar of passing buses. Then, in a small, careful voice, Jacky told me that Bobbie's father had died the night before. Bobbie was a mutual friend, an artist who lived in a loft a few blocks from my house. Her father had been ill with cancer for several months. The three of us knew one another through the Vancouver art community; coincidentally or not, we were also all queer—lesbian, bi, and transgendered—and all of Ukrainian descent.

"I'll have a barbecue," I said reflexively. "You and Bobbie will come." "OK," said Jacky. She knew better than to argue when I got it into my head to have a dinner party. I joined Jacky on her trip to Hellsgate to buy groceries. There in the mall was Bobbie, emerging from the liquor store, arms laden with vodka and whiskey, a confused look in her big brown eyes.

I knew immediately I would make chicken, the ultimate comfort food. My mother's fried chicken cured homesickness on parent's day at summer camp. Baba's chicken stew summed up all the pleasure of being a child at her house, of idle afternoons watching *People's Court*. With such minimal lead-time, shortcuts were more than justified. I would buy a jar of prepared barbecue sauce and add puréed garlic and ginger (also from jars), mashed chipotle in adobe sauce, and fresh-squeezed lime juice. A bit of brown sugar or maple syrup to taste, and *voilà*, a sweet and spicy sauce that would form a rich, syrupy crust on the chicken. I walked through Buy-Lo, the decidedly unglamorous supermarket attached to Hellsgate, and pondered the array of summer produce. Fresh romaine and a hunk of Parmesan in my kitchen inspired a Caesar salad. I decided to make grilled yams too, a favourite of Bobbie's.

Some meals are spontaneous, others recurring as planned, over and over again. Like a train's evening whistle, there is both beauty and a kind of unnamable sadness in such a routine. Lesya's mom's roast chicken was like that. Lesya and I grew up together, enduring the same Ukrainian language schools and summer camps: hours of shared boredom in church basements or amidst remote Canadian landscapes. When I was a teenager, Lesya's narrow two-storey brick house was a refuge for me, a hideout from the sterile suburbs and their unreasonable expectations. I always stretched out my welcome as far as I possibly could, arriving for dinner and remaining until lunch the next day. Mornings, her taciturn, bemused father would serve us *challah* toast with rosehip jam and milky coffee, a meal that naturally evolved into lunch, cooked by her mother: *mamalega* (polenta) and roast chicken.

Lesya's mama would spin out breathtaking adventure stories as she stirred the cornmeal into boiling chicken broth. Her tiny, round body was hardly bigger than the stove; her face, with its beautifully chiseled cheekbones and high forehead, was flushed with heat and a dark kind of pleasure. She told us about being a prisoner of war in the Ural Mountains while barely out of her teens, signalling for trains on some windswept Russian plain. Her voice was sorrowful and proud as she described how she was then captured by the Germans and sent to Occupied France to cook for the Nazis in a labour camp. It was a horrible job: any misstep in flavouring could cost her her life. Then she unspooled her long, sad tales of immigration: the pain they'd left behind, the pain they'd discovered here. Lesya and I calmly chewed our *challah* toast as her mama's voice took on a keening, remorseful tone. It was the soundtrack of our childhoods. It was tragic, but we were used to it. I felt as though I'd heard all of these stories, or their variations, before: from my father or his long-faced refugee friends. They were as much a part of my life as television and summer camp. As I listened to Lesya's mom, my mouth watered, anticipating the soft, luscious polenta, which would be topped with bacon, and then juxtaposed against the crispy skin and tender meat of the chicken. It was good, basic Ukrainian Sunday-dinner cuisine, food that made you feel like you belonged somewhere.

My dinner with Jacky and Bobbie took place under a dark blue summer sky, the day's heat slowly receding. We toasted to her father Nestor's memory with vodka, and then again with the sticky Hungarian wine Jacky had brought. Bobbie told us that as her father lay dying, she decided to build a wheelchair ramp for him so he could go outside. Nestor only used the ramp once, when Bobbie took him out to see the stars puncturing the sky over the Rocky Mountains. She stopped being a girl during that time, wore boy's clothes and did manly things with hammer and drill. It was a father-son moment; a generous return to lost origins; an ironic pretense; a final gift to his dad.

I had prepared a large amount of barbecued chicken, planning for leftovers, but it all got eaten. Just like me when my father died, Bobbie was furiously hungry. She had seconds and then thirds, of everything. The chicken was tangy, sweet, and slightly charred. The yams had been coated in olive oil, lime, and rosemary, quartered, and then grilled; soft on the inside, crisp on the outside. I passed around garlic-basil mayonnaise to dip them into. I talked about my father, what it was like when he died, how I felt relief and then anger, and then, months later, a long, unspeakable sadness. No matter what your relationship with your parents, their passing creates an absence that aches in its own insistent way. We talked about the importance of funerals, where you meet long-lost uncles and cousins, and hear stories that subtly change the shape of your memories. Being Ukrainian, we were used to conversations about death, where you eat and drink and even laugh with extravagance, amid the spirits of those who have gone ahead.

I don't know the exact recipe for Lesya's mom's chicken, its falling-off-the-bone goodness. I assume that it was seasoned simply, with only salt, pepper, and paprika. I suspect that melted butter was brushed onto the skin. I know it probably baked slowly, at low heat, long enough for Lesya and I to squander an entire morning in her small, warm kitchen, still clad in our nightgowns, in the languid manner of teenagers. Long enough for her mama to tell us more stories, then go to church and come back, serving the chicken and *mamalega* to us grandly in the dining room.

But I know the recipes for comfort, for mourning, and for celebration. I knew, even then, that it was all of a piece: the sadness and longing of our elders; the nearness of death; the deep pleasure of tradition; and the comforts of a meal of roast chicken and friends who were, in some wide, tribal sense, family.

FOOD VOYAGES

There is a streak of wanderlust in my family. Travel, almost always to Europe, was at the centre of my father's life and, much later, central to my own. Travelling is a fine line: are you running towards something, or running away? I didn't really understand the academic business that took *Tato* to London, Rome, and Cologne, leaving us and our mother behind, only that he was sure to return with fantastic trinkets and fantastically boring Super 8 films.

The first thing I did when I got out of high school was to purchase a charter flight to Europe, $125 return, good for a year. I can still remember the delicious, foreboding feeling that ticket gave me, sitting in my purse like a time bomb. I took along an enormous orange knapsack with a Canadian flag sewn onto it, a Eurail Pass, a wad of American Express traveller's cheques, and my square Ukrainian Canadian girlfriends, Nadia and Anna-Lisa. Desperate to run away, we found ourselves, on that trip, back home in Ukraine. We mostly stayed at convents—my father's ingenious idea. Those chilly, high-ceilinged nunneries smelled of cabbage and beef, just like Baba's kitchen. There were always rules, many of them unspoken: delicate as linen, confining as iron bars. You had to be back for dinner, you had to be quiet while you ate, and the doors were locked and bolted by ten. I got reacquainted with Europe through a protective veil of lace curtains and Catholic ritual. In Rome, we finally rebelled, eschewing the starchy convent meals served at a long refectory table in the company of clinically depressed visiting priests. Instead, we wandered the streets and parks with reckless abandon, singing, flirting with

Italian boys, nibbling on crusty bread and ricotta cheese, taking long, lusty swigs from a bottle of Cinzano concealed in a paper bag. Nadia's long Ukrainian braid got loose and untidy; Anna Lisa released her waist-length blonde hair from its tight clips and let it float like a cloud across her shoulders, driving the Italian boys wild. I could feel our propriety fleeing from us, like a sweater caught up in a drift of wind.

Travelling, I learned how to cook. I watched what French women bought at markets in small towns, asked nosy questions about the food that was offered to me by friends met along the way. I returned to my mother's kitchen and attempted omelette au fromage, salade niçoise, crêpes, quiche Lorraine. I affected European airs, taking my café au lait only in a bowl, wearing my scarves a certain way, melodramatically lamenting the inferior quality of Canadian cheese, pastry, and baguette.

At the age of twenty-one, I returned to Europe with a slightly crazy girl, Tamara. She was the only person I could find mad enough to hitchhike with me along autobahns and autoroutes, one of us wielding a handmade sign that said Paris, or Burgundy, or Genève. Travelling on the cheap, we always carried a net bag of spices, garlic, and tomato paste. Arriving late and hungry to a hostel, and with a last-minute purchase of local wine, vegetables, and pasta, we could throw together a meal in fifteen minutes. Boys hovered around us like hungry fruit flies.

Travelling, I learned how to improvise, like a singer who left her score at home: to deepen the notes of a tomato sauce with a whisper of anchovy, or a dash of red wine; paprika and Toulouse sausage to liven up last night's ratatouille, scooped up with torn pieces of fresh *pain de campagne*.

One rainy day in an eastern province of France found us, at twilight, hitching to get to a hostel somewhere in the Swiss Alps. A somber man in a tweed suit and a cap picked us up, very Jacques Tati. When we told him where we were going, he shrugged noncommittally. When we asked him where he was going, he shrugged again. It was a dodgy situation, the kind that gave our mothers nightmares. Thus began a harrowing journey up narrow Alpine highways, with regular stops for *une verre du rouge* along the way. Mist and a damp, melancholy darkness descended on the road; we lost our way several times. You had to be in your early twenties, really, to endure such a journey. Finally, we arrived at the remote Alpine hostel. Even though it was past midnight, a buxom woman in an apron quietly prepared us a meal. It was a simple repast of crêpes au fromage, accompanied by the usual glass of local red wine. We fell hungrily upon the food, savouring the woodsy taste of Emmenthal, the sweetness of the crêpes. Out of the corner of my eye I watched our new companion, who had told us only his first name, Michel. He was wiping cheese off his plate with a heel of bread; he looked happy for the first time since we'd met. Had he come all this way on a lonely night just to be able to share a meal?

The hostel was tiny, and there was only one room with two beds left. Tamara and I shared a bed, and Michel took the other. I fell fast asleep. At dawn, I awoke suddenly. Michel was bending over me. A scream tried to hurl itself out of my throat. But no, Michel was pulling photos out of his wallet: two kids and a wife standing in front of a small house—happy, normal-looking, boring. *Je m'en vais* (I'm on my way) was all he said, and then he was gone.

Travelling is a fine line. Do you travel to improve upon the taste of food you cook at home? Or is travelling a means to savour illicit flavours, to taste spice and tannin and sweetness unimaginable to your family and friends?

PRANZO

I arrived late at night, after seventeen hours of travel including stopovers. It was ten days before Easter. A pleasant young man holding a sign with my name misspelled on it met me at the airport and deposited me at a shabby, spooky hotel. I boarded an ancient wrought-iron lift that took me and my luggage to a small room with an oversized oak bureau and a narrow single bed. I inserted myself between the crisp, tight sheets. I resolved to spend most of my time sequestered in that room, writing and sleeping.

I was in Turin, Italy, the country's centre for auto manufacturing and home to The Shroud. I was there as a guest of the Turin lesbian and gay film festival. I knew no one who had included Turin on any of their Italian itineraries: I expected churches and car dealerships and little else.

I was forty-two years old. I'd been to so many queer and women's film festivals in the past decade, each with their own charm and privilege, but too often short on certain essentials. I'd slept on floors and couches, subsisted on chocolate bars, gin and tonics, and the distracted attentions of volunteers. My eyes burned all the time with fatigue and the dazzle of foreign landscapes. Surrounded by colleagues and audiences, I often felt lonely. Was I turning into a version of my father? Someone whose suitcase was constantly being emptied or filled; someone who was often away for their friends' birthdays or family gatherings; someone who *wasn't there*.

Once, at a film festival in Amsterdam, all of the filmmakers were invited to the gala opening banquet. We got dressed up and styled our hair, excited to be wined and dined. It soon became apparent, however, that no tables had been reserved for us. Every last chair had been taken by city dignitaries and their fur-clad wives. Almost without a word, we agreed to leave en masse, a weaving line of black leather jackets. What I remember from that night is not so much the revolutionary act itself, largely unnoticed—but that we went to a cheap Indonesian restaurant, where we shared a delicious *rijstaffel*: a long narrow platform placed across the middle of our table, heated by candles, and set with small bowls of curries, sambals, fruit, satay, peanuts, boiled eggs, and rice. We ate voraciously and talked for hours: about our work, about the heartaches and pleasures of being independent filmmakers, about our celluloid dreams.

Turin changed everything, and all because of *pranzo*.

I woke up, my first morning in Turin, to lines of yellow buttery light filtering through shutters. Like a character in a 1950s Italian movie, I threw open the shutters to a courtyard lined with ochre walls, dozens of clotheslines, and a hundred lives.

Breakfast in the hotel's dim basement dining room was a weary affair: oddly textured rolls, pots of yogurt, little containers of jam. I spotted some other filmmakers and sat down at their table. There was Matteo, a sweet-faced writer from Milan; Yvonne, an intense, witty filmmaker from Dublin, petite as a doll; André, a tall, goateed programmer from São Paolo; and Bavo, a Belgian director, bland and good-humoured. The film festival was happening miles away on the outskirts of town, but no one seemed to be making any effort to get there. Instead, everyone seemed obsessed about *pranzo*, or lunch: who would be there, what food would be served. It was decided we'd all go shopping and head back to the hotel by noon. Delighted to be in the company of people for whom the day's second meal mattered so very much, I eagerly joined their ranks.

We emerged onto streets rich with baroque architecture and humming with life. The air smelled of exhaust, espresso, and chocolate. Gelaterias, shoe stores, and coffee bars vied for customers. Matteo, playing tour guide, officiously informed us that Turin was the first capital of Italy, back in the nineteenth century. Kilometres of arcades dating back 200 years sheltered all the main streets; ornate wrought iron gates opened onto exquisite courtyards with fountains and gardens. There wasn't a car dealership in sight.

At exactly one p.m., a white minibus showed up at the hotel's front door. We crammed ourselves in and headed to La Reseda, a restaurant owned by the festival director's partner. There, in a wide sunny room, seated at long tables anchored with baskets of *pane* and jugs of *vino rosso y bianco*, were film festival staff and volunteers, as well as all of the visiting film-makers. It was a scene that touched my soul. For several hours each day, no films were screened and the festival offices were closed. *Pranzo.*

There was a luxurious pace to those festival lunches, with their three different courses, or *piatti*, and bottomless terra-cotta jugs of wine. Indeed, it was in this very region that the slow food movement had been invented. Turin is located in the province of Piedmont, bordering on Switzerland; on a clear day, you could see the Alps in the distance. The cuisine of the region has a northern feel, simple but refined. Breadsticks originated in Turin, as did vermouth: rice and truffles are grown in abundance. The mozzarella, tomato sauce, and garlic-laden dishes that made up my repertoire of Italian cooking were no-where in evidence. Instead, a typical lunch menu consisted of an appetizer risotto containing nuts and gorgonzola, followed by a grilled filet of salmon marinated in olive oil and capers, and concluded with *insalada mixta* (mixed greens) dressed with olive oil and vinegar placed in bottles at the table. Dessert was elementary as well, lemon gelato with *fragola* (strawberries), or a cheese plate.

The grilled fish and chicken I ate that week were a revelation: that meat and fish could be so plainspoken, no sauce to obscure their fresh, clean flavour. We laughed a lot during those lunches. Yvonne flirted shamelessly with all of the waitresses, and I became acquainted with a sweet coterie of local gay Italian men, who flirted shamelessly with me. My loneliness slipped quietly away.

Matteo, Yvonne, Andre, Bavo, and myself quickly became a temporary queer family. They insisted on supervising my quest for an Italian leather jacket; Andre and Bavo were apoplectic when I refused to purchase one in lavender, a shade that was all the rage in Italy that spring. Within days, the five of us were making absurd, fantastical plans to spend the following Christmas together. Matteo said that in Italy there is a saying, "Christmas with family, Easter with friends." We decided to invert the equation.

Matteo was my favourite of all my new acquaintances, a gentle, considerate, middle-aged gay novelist, always clad in the same dowdy tweed sports coat. A respected Milanese literary figure, he'd been invited by the festival to sit on one of its juries. In the wee hours, I'd huddle with Matteo in a corner of some gay bar in downtown Turin, sipping Campari. We talked about relationships: Matteo was in a loving and steady partnership, while mine, with Krys, seemed to be unraveling. I told him about Krys's intermittent bouts of illness during which she often got angry at me. Matteo said thoughtfully, tenderly: "You have to find a way to be supportive, but also you have to protect yourself." We talked about writing, about being rejected by our families for being queer, and about the latest episodes of *ER*, which had just started to appear on Italian TV. (Would Dr. Carrie *ever* come out?) It was so uncanny, and so comforting, to trace the similar contours of a lesbian and gay life across international borders. I'd slip away at two in the morning to walk the glittery cobblestones back to the hotel, stopping at a tiny perfect *gelateria* for a cone of something that was the exact taste of fresh raspberries on a summer's day. I caught myself thinking, for the first time in a long while: *life is good*.

After the festival was over, I planned to travel along the southwestern coast of Italy for a few days during the Easter holiday. Much to my surprise, I discovered that all of Italy travels at that time. Every single hotel in the country was absolutely full. Matteo quietly placed a call of his own. Two days later, I was in Genoa, staying at the tiny, airy apartment of his sister Francesca.

Genoa is sultry, slutty Mediterranean counterpoint to Turin's sophisticated cool. It is the capital of Liguria, and straddles part of the Italian Riviera, evoking 1960s Gina Lollobrigida movies and Alpha Romeo convertibles shooting along narrow coastal roads.

Francesca, gamine and charming, welcomed me wholeheartedly into her world. Her apartment was full of books on new wave cinema. She was besotted with Godard and could recite the holy names of all his films, like a rosary. She'd meet up with me at lunch and we'd take coffee the way Italians do: three or four quick sips of thick tangy espresso while standing at the bar. After she went back to work, I explored Genoa on foot, threading my way along dark, medieval streets lined with tiny shops specializing in everything from tripe to hardware items to pasta. I discovered that pesto is Liguria's signature dish, but I also encountered memorable fish markedly different in style from the Piemontese, like the grilled cod with curried mayonnaise at some hole-in-the-wall Francesca led me to. We talked endlessly about movies, Francesca's eyes full of ardor and passion. Every night she'd make up her sofa bed for me, and would herself sleep on a roll-out cot alongside. It was innocent and intimate, like we were sisters.

I left Genoa on Easter Sunday, as church bells tolled across the city and girls in their best print dresses walked with their families to visit friends, carrying *paloma*, the traditional dove-shaped Easter bread. Whatever had turned bitter in my heart had sweetened. For days afterwards, when I was back in Canada, all I could hear was opera music, and all I could smell was espresso and chocolate, with a side of good Italian car exhaust.

My trip to Italy, seductive and exotic as it was, had only worked to strengthen the flavours of home. A restaurant with terracotta tile floors in northern Italy; a bistro table on a thin patch of grass in my backyard in Vancouver, beneath a gnarled misshapen apple tree. All of it is home, but the road there appears and disappears—so that it's only the smell of cooking food that points you in the direction of where you came from, and who you need to be.

MEZE

I once met a cook, a short, compact man with eyes as deep and brown as Turkish coffee, and a heart as wide as the Aegean sea. It took me a day, and a night, and another day of travel on various crowded buses to get to his village on the western coast of Turkey, a place touted in my guidebook as being well off the beaten track, and said to be possessed of no small amount of charm.

It was just a year after my trip to Italy, and I found myself travelling again. I had, in that space of time, begun doctoral studies. Eight months of coursework and all of the dry, deferential behaviours required of a PhD candidate evoked in me a restless thirst for travel. I found a conference tangentially related to my research, in Izmir, on the western coast of Turkey. After convincing various bemused department chairs of the urgency of such a scholarly voyage, I managed to obtain sufficient funds. I decided to take two weeks to get to Izmir from Istanbul, via a complicated overland route, across the historic plains of Anatolia on Turkey's mainland. I imagined a romantic journey in a gracefully-appointed train carriage, Orient Express-style, sipping Turkish coffee as meadows and mountains flew by. Upon further examination, however, I realized I would instead be lurching across the country by bus.

Train travel is an inefficient option in Turkey. Historically controlled by foreign military interests, the rail lines are circuitous and intermittent, built to avoid naval fire (thus, there are no coastal trains), or to strategically divert the enemy (no direct routes, either). So, if you want to get anywhere in Turkey, you will most likely take a bus and, for reasons unknown, it is fairly certain that it will leave at midnight.

Buses in Turkey are a culture unto themselves. They are housed in *otogars*, bus stations as expansive as airports, with enormous mezzanines and a variety of ways to obtain tea, but little else. Despite the lateness of the hour, the *otogar* will be full of people, and full of a bewildering array of choices: there are thirty or forty private bus companies in Turkey, all of them tracing the same routes. You will attempt to comparison-shop your fare, politely inquiring at one company and then another, making of yourself a pleasing spectacle for the men at every booth. Everyone will say that their route is "*direkt*" and since the word for direct is the same in Turkish as in English, and since you have no other choice, you will believe them.

The bus will be as crowded and lively as though it were the middle of the day. If you are a woman travelling alone, you will tire of men's gazes, full of both hostility and expectation, constantly caressing your skin. You will be grateful for the custom of seating women with women, men with men. The woman next to you will most likely be veiled, and more often than not, she will have a small child on her lap. The woman will smile shyly at you, but the child will not; you will share with them the dried Turkish apricots and Swiss chocolate you always carry with you. The bus will leave promptly; there will be Turkish music jangling out of the bus's speakers. The bus driver's assistant will pass through proffering lemon cologne, and you will watch as everyone carefully washes their hands and faces with it. Later, and with great ceremony, Nescafé and water will be served to all.

The windows will be dark velvet oblongs. You will feel as though you are the middle of nowhere; you are, in fact, in the very heart of Turkey, traversing the wide, primordial Anatolian plain, birthplace of several civilizations. You will sleep fit-fully, dreaming of ancient caravans, floating in a blur of Slavic and Middle Eastern words and images. There will be frequent, middle-of-the-night shopping stops at roadside emporiums offering Turkish Delight, kebabs, and *kylyms* that look just like the ones you've seen hanging in your great aunt Olena's home. At each stop, the bus's exterior will be hosed down, and water will stream across your window like tears.

You will wake up again as dawn illuminates rounded blue mountains. Unknown sage-green rivers will pass by your window, and the slow-motion, early morning movements of villagers carrying loaves of bread, sending children off to school, or glancing up from cafés will stir you to wonder. Like Cyrus, sixth-century emperor of Persia, like the nineteenth-century German and British adventurers before you, you have come to the very edge of Anatolia after quenching your thirst for history and novelty at its core. You resemble them in some ways, although you are neither a conquerer nor a plunderer, not exactly.

You will arrive in the middle of a sun-bleached May morning, at a destination that is *not* the one written on your ticket. Your bag will be unloaded efficiently off the bus and you will stand dazed amid a crowd of equally confused Australian backpackers. It will dawn on you that there is no *direkt* bus to your village, never has been. You will obtain some Turkish coffee, and a sweet bun, to give you strength. You will haul yourself and your luggage on and off buses for the better part of the day, after which you will hike 3.5 kilometres to get to your precious village.

It was the cook who greeted me when I arrived, dusty and exhausted, at my pension. My guidebook decreed that this was the most hospitable place to stay in the entire village of Patara.

The village itself had an abandoned, sinister feel. Signs advertising various brands of mosquito repellent were prominent along the main drag, as were countless portraits of Santa Claus. I found out later that Patara was the birthplace of St Nicholas, that legendary fourth-century Byzantine bishop, and that by mid-summer, the place becomes infested with mosquitos.

The pension was almost completely occupied by Dutch tourists. They returned with great merriment that evening from a tour to nearby Greek ruins, organized by the proprietor. Amid a hubbub of Dutch conversation, I sat alone at my table, under the grape arbor sheltering the terrace. I re-read the guidebook, trying to discern what it was about this village that had so charmed its authors and, indeed, half the citizens of Holland. I was seriously considering heading off the next morning when a basket of warm crusty bread kissed with olive oil, garlic, and fresh oregano arrived with my glass of Turkish wine. While good white bread is plentiful in Turkey, I had never once seen it adorned in this way. I had ordered only an entrée—*karides güveç*, a prawn casserole—but a *meze* of warm green and white beans dressed with a lemony tomato sauce appeared in front of me. I shook my head, thinking the waiter had made a mistake, but he shrugged resignedly and nodded his head in the direction of the kitchen.

Turkish food is one of the world's most venerable cuisines. Eggplant, tomatoes, rice, beans, lamb, and chicken form the foundation of many succulent and varied dishes. Irfan Orga, author of *Turkish Cooking*, goes so far as to boast, "Turks have always eaten better than any other people in the Eastern Mediterranean." He describes the lavish Sultan's feasts of the Ottoman Empire, featuring such dishes as "young suckling calf stuffed with rice and exotic herbs ... kidneys ravished in sour cream, kebabs wrapped in paper and cooked with pine kernels." Orga insists upon the extravagance of his country's food: "*Dolmas* (grape leaves filled with rice and meat) are heavy with stuffing … meats, braised or grilled or cooked with a vegetable, often come to the table swimming in butter or sheep's fat." And yet, for most of my time in Turkey thus far, I had found only the most straightforward of foods: fish grilled with lemon and olive oil; chicken kebab, similarly dressed, and served with pilav. All delicious, but plain and repetitive. Traditional Ottoman delicacies were, it seemed, being cooked only in private homes. People had advised me to stick to *meze* but this was the first time I'd found appetizers as tempting as this. The prawn casserole that followed held the lushness I'd been longing for, with its creamy sheep's milk cheese topping, its rich, garlicky tomato sauce coating a multitude of fresh prawns.

The next day, I tried to join one of the tours for which the pension was known. I was interested in going to nearby Xanthos, with its Lycian pillar tombs. I spoke with the proprietor, who gravely assured me that there was no tour that day, but that there would surely be one the next. I asked him if there was a bus going to the beach, and again he said, no, no, not that day, but perhaps the next.

I began the long hot walk to the coast, a route which meandered through fields of poppies studded with fifth-century ruins. This entire region had once been the domain of the Lycians, an indigenous people with a penchant for mortuaries. I wandered through a triumphal gate, examined the necropolis, the ubiquitous, elaborate tombs, and a lovely half-moon of a theatre, silted with sand. When a van with my pension's name on it passed by, full of Dutch citizens, I took no offense. I ended the afternoon lying on hot, white sand and swimming in the turquoise Aegean sea.

Later, trudging home through a gilded twilight, I mused upon the varieties and hierarchies of western tourists to this country. The Dutch seemed to take naturally to being served by the Turkish people; took to it with the easy charm and grace that is the vernacular of privilege. Indeed, Holland is home to thousands of Turkish immigrants, where they form a distinct underclass. I, with my olive skin and un-western name, became in Turkey a lesser sort of tourist, something I secretly prided myself on. But for the moment I was hungry and my feet ached. It suddenly rankled not to have that blonde, breezy sense of luxury.

That evening, more symbolic redress from the cook. A procession of *meze* arrived, unbidden, at my table. Tomatoes stuffed with herbed rice and currants; *dolmas* pierced with the flavours of lamb and nutmeg; broad beans commingling with the complementary languages of local olive oil and mint. I ordered a second glass of wine to wash them down. The waiter, exasperated, came by my table to let me know that the cook was also offering his services as a masseur. I demurred, but after dinner went to the kitchen to thank him, and to shake his hand. He looked at me with tired, liquid eyes and shrugged, modestly, gracefully.

I spent my last morning at the beach, surfing the waves, lying in the sand. For lunch, I ate *manti*, a kind of ravioli stuffed with minced lamb and coated with a yogurt-mint sauce, at a small, dour, family-run café. I returned to the pension in good time to meet with the proprietor, who had promised to drive me to the bus stop almost four kilometres away. But it was the cook who met me, with a pained expression on his face. It turned out that the proprietor had whisked the Dutch people away to Xanthos for an impromptu tour, and there was to be no ride. He wrung his hands and then ran to get my bags. As he hailed a taxi for me, I looked one last time into his eyes and saw a sweet, deep brew of shyness and longing there. I held his hand for a moment, and then got into the cab.

I continued my bus voyage along the curvaceous, frilly edge of the Aegean, my tongue experimenting with the sound of place names: Dalyan, Marmaris, Kusadesi, Izmir. The food became more familiar somehow, with echoes of Greece, undertones of Italy. I ate dried figs and dates purchased at food stalls along the way; had breakfasts of fresh tomatoes, feta cheese, Tauros mountain honey, and olives; snacked on roasted chickpeas and *halvah*. Moving as far west as is possible in Turkey, the women's veils started to disappear, and I was intrigued by the sight of one or two young Turkish women, never more, travelling on their own.

I arrived to meet academic colleagues in Izmir, the birthplace of Homer. This marked the end of my epic odyssey as a solo traveller. With these new friends I shared meals of beef kebab, arugula salad, grilled mackerel, yogurt with cucumber, stuffed squid. We drank *raki*, Turkey's anise-flavoured national drink, and it set all of us to dancing.

I returned by night bus to Istanbul to catch my plane to Vancouver, via London. Boarding an early morning ferry for the Asian side of Istanbul, I watched in awe as swallows traced uneven arcs of flight across the ferry's wake, and the spires of the Blue Mosque and the Aya Sophia embroidered the horizon. White sunlight danced upon the blue sheen of the Bosphorus, the body of water that divides Europe from Asia and flows into the Black Sea. If I followed the oily, churning current of those waters, I would eventually find myself in Ukraine, headwaters of my own byzantine ancestral origins. Traveller without a single root, with a confusion of destinations, I am always sailing to, and from, Byzantium.

FISH ON FRIDAYS

Growing up in a Catholic family, I grew accustomed to fish on Fridays. It was part of a culture that was part of me: prayer cards that smelled of *eau de cologne*, tucked into the corners of my mother's vanity mirror; at church, a larger-than-life portrait of a bleeding Jesus, draped over a coffin-sized box whose wounds we had to kiss on Good Friday. At the age of seven or eight, thinking up sins to recite in confession to a surly priest huddled behind a screen. Premature lessons in existentialism, as when Sister Frances drew a single small dot on the blackboard and announced, to her awestruck Grade One class, as blithely as though teaching the alphabet: "That dot is your life. The rest, children, is eternity."

Fish on Fridays was a Sacrifice, something to do with Jesus and All His Suffering, or so we were told by Sister Frances. So every other Friday, Mama breaded whitefish or cod fillets in milk, then egg, then breadcrumbs, and fried them in oil; occasionally, we ate them with fried potatoes, a mound of greyish canned beans on the side. On Fridays in between, we ate pickled herring with baked potatoes. The combination of the tart herrings—and the way they slid silkily down the throat—with the stolid, chalky taste of potatoes topped with sweet butter was essential: on their own, neither would have appealed. Fish on Fridays was no big sacrifice. It was always delicious, and made us feel more Catholic in a superior, cliquish way.

When I moved to the west coast, I found myself eating less

fish than I'd expected to. Except for the ubiquitous sushi, fish in Vancouver is somewhat of a luxury, something for a posh evening out. But it was on a conference trip back to Halifax on the east coast of Canada, where I once lived, that I rediscovered the delights of fish on Friday—and every other day.

You notice the impoverishment as soon as you get off the plane. There is something old, something slow, about this region that is bittersweet. The airport shuttle is a renovated schoolbus. It takes you along a highway that is secretively, darkly rural, lakes glinting like old copper coins along the way.

Between conference sessions that week, I manage to eat a lot of fish, wanting to try it in all its forms. From a takeout place at the refurbished dock known as Historic Properties, I have grilled Atlantic salmon as I have never eaten it, wrapped in a pita with tzatziki, lettuce, and tomato. At Soho Kitchen, an informal café with gold and green walls, I savour cornmeal-crusted halibut with mango salsa, washed down by good, spicy conversation with Dorota, a brilliant Polish–Canadian academic specializing in trauma theory.

One evening, drained by days of presentations with such overwrought titles as "The Unqueering of Chicago" and "Twentieth-Century Theoretical Development and the Decline of the Father," I return, headachy, to my friend Pat's house, thinking I will simply go to bed early. But this is Nova Scotia, after all: she and her friend Jerry drag me to the local pub. The kitchen is run by a robust Greek woman who seems to know everyone's name. She cooks up grilled halibut for me, fried Digby clams and chips for Jerry and Pat. My halibut tastes of lemon and olive oil, and of Greek Islands in the sun. Jerry raves about his clams, says you can't get them fried up whole like that anymore.

Another day, my fellow graduate student Joanna and I

play hookey from the conference and take a drive up the South Shore. In the chaos of lost maps and half-remembered instructions, we manage to get out past the roundabouts for which Halifax is famous and suddenly find ourselves in the country. We spend the day driving along lyrical, winding old highways as pine trees, scrub, and tea shops unravel alongside. I want Joanna to see a real, unspoiled fishing village, so we detour to Lower Prospect. The village rises up from the road in dreamy shades of grey and blue: clapboard houses, fishing shacks, a few lobster pots; and the pure white of ocean spray from waves that rise defiantly, metres high. We drop in on craftspeople selling wares whose designs go back centuries: quilts, knitted socks, hooked rugs. I marvel at how undeveloped the South Shore still is, how unchanged since I, a young art student, hitchhiked along its roads. But everything that is quaint and picturesque is everything that makes life difficult here. Depleting fish stocks and unemployment have marked and scarred people's lives.

The gustatory highlight of the day is our meal at Peggy's Cove. Most people would not expect to dine well, and so cheaply, at such a popular tourist attraction. The extent to which the lowly lobster has been enshrined—as keychain, ashtray, salt and pepper shaker, fridge magnet, wall plaque, snow globe, and oven mitt—might overwhelm them, and they might be inclined to head directly back to the pristine safety of their rental car and drive on. But they would be missing something very fine.

A Nova Scotian professor had strongly suggested that, were I to visit Peggy's Cove, the fish hash would be the thing to order, and so I do. Fish hash is really nothing more than mashed potatoes with bits of haddock and fried onion mixed in: slightly sweet, slightly salty. But it is in the combination of flavours that this dish transcends the sum of its parts, for it comes accompanied by green tomato chow and baked beans.

The beans have a deep, dusky taste, accented with molasses and pork. The chow, a kind of chutney, is both syrupy and tart. It is a wonderful mélange of tastes, held together by tradition. Joanna, who is of Scottish/Irish descent, surmises that this dish probably dates back to the days of the British Empire, when ships arrived back from the Indian colonies full of condiments discovered on the subcontinent. But fish hash, I learn later, also appears in ancient Jewish lore: a simple food one can prepare easily on Shabbat. In one story I've read, fish hash symbolizes *Oneg Shabbat*—enjoyment of the Sabbath, despite its prohibitions.

For dessert, Joanna and I share a dish of warm ginger-bread, fragrant with cardamom and molasses, topped with whipped cream. Joanna is transported back to her last visit to Scotland, but I flashback to this same place, twenty-five years earlier. I remember hitchhiking numerous times to Peggy's Cove with art school friends, always on a whim. All we could ever afford was the hot gingerbread, split several ways, and a pot of tea. Then we'd go and roam the rocks, making art with pencils, cameras, and paintbrushes: swirling waves, tilted pastel houses, the bleak, forceful line of stone against sea. Curled up against the granite with my sketchbook, I drew with desperation until it was time to head back to the highway. Art saved me, as it had my father, but in a different way. Going off to a small art school on the far-away coast of Nova Scotia was how I managed to escape the sweet, sticky demands of femininity in my world: fish on Fridays, church on Sunday, every week, every month, every year.

My own culinary traditions and ritual foods were born on this jagged piece of coast. I'd never eaten a turnip or a squash until I moved to the east coast, foods too reminiscent of trauma to be allowed in my parents' home. I savoured miso, and tahini, and brown rice for the first time. Food was only part of the story, but it symbolized various forms of liberation: vegetarian soups that could feed a tableful of artist-housemates or an entire lesbian-feminist collective; produce and cheese from a food co-op; recipe books that reminded you of the planet you were on and your responsibility to it.

Sated, Joanna and I return to the present, pay the bill and get back on the road. The only regrettable thing about our lunch is that we are unable to eat for hours afterwards. Signs advertising lobster rolls, chowders and pies, forlornly pass us by. Thankfully, our hunger eventually returns, just in time for dinner at Jim's.

Jim is an old friend from art school days. He was also my first gay male friend and, with his sense of dignity, social justice, and giggly high humour, set my standards for all the rest. As long as I've known him, Jim has lived on Brunswick Street in Halifax's North End in a tall, ramshackle nineteenth-century house he owns with four other artists. I've eaten many meals there, and gotten stoned just as often, in the huge basement kitchen of the house, its dormer windows overlooking the harbour. People drift in willy-nilly and it takes you all evening to figure out who's lovers with who, whose kids are whose: an amicable smorgasbord of relationships and co-operative child-rearing, everyone making it up as they go along.

Judith, a visiting filmmaker from Toronto, is busy marinating asparagus spears when we arrive, and then moves on to bread several pounds of scallops. I lay out an appetizer platter of smoked halibut, mackerel, and salmon, purchased from a supermarket in Chester. Dinner is a deliciously mismatched potluck: garlic pasta and fried scallops; Andreas' spicy baked chicken; Jim's gigantic salad. As we indulge in the sweet, soft scallops and throw back glass after glass of cheap Italian wine, I watch as a transformative exchange of ideas—about film, about theories gleaned at the conference, about the checkered history of this house—intensifies across Jim's well-worn kitchen table.

Leaving Halifax a few days later, I buy a few pounds of smoked fish from a fish shop conveniently located in the airport and share it with my sister Lydia in Ottawa, my next stop. The flavours are intense: pepper, maple syrup, lemon. The memories it evokes are no less vivid: the smoky, earthy taste of Nova Scotian friendships stays with me long after the fish is devoured.

FOOD FOR THE BODY

Food was never an uncomplicated thing in my family. Food as reward, food as punishment, food as ritual. Contradictions were as plentiful as the rye bread that appeared at every meal. My mother, not thin but not fat either, cooked six extravagant dinners per week—and was always on a diet. As a kid, I considered my mother beautiful; the graceful, dark-haired woman with high cheekbones and shy smile, endlessly documented in the home movies, was imprinted on my memory, no need for touch-ups. But we never saw her touch the sweet and sour meatballs, the homemade sauerkraut with garlic sausage, the apple pie. Did she come right out and tell us, her daughters, that we were fat too, or did we simply absorb an idea of corpulence, of our teenage bodies being ugly, unruly, even frightening?

Sometimes I caught glimpses of my father's rolls of flesh at the beach, or through the open bedroom door—pale, forbidden, oddly feminine. Flesh of my flesh. Was it his body or mine that frightened me more? My body, newly sexed but not yet sexual, was hardening in odd places, softening in others. Why was I—not thin but not fat at age fifteen—boiling a single grey wiener at lunch, to be eaten with melba toast? At dinner, huge servings of scalloped potatoes with fried pork chops would appear, my mother a nervous shadow behind the kitchen counter. My father, rotund, hedonistic, would have two helpings, followed by dessert and a cheese plate. I danced my fork around the potatoes, cut the golden rind of fat off the chops, sanctimoniously spooned my mother's saccharin into my tea. I weighed myself daily, waiting for something to change. My body, a stranger to me; my body, that would surely turn against me.

I never lost weight, but never gained any either. Those Anglo suburbs were so quiet and chilly; muffled voices behind hedges; well-dressed English-speaking families neatly getting in and out of cars. Sensory pleasures were scarce amid the cookie cutter sameness of aluminium siding and faux shutters. Food—the aroma of stewing pork hocks; the tangy smell of rhubarb pie—seemed to be the only thing that helped me understand who I was and why I was there, so far away from the place our immigrant parents still referred to as "home."

It took me years to understand food's elemental connection to the body. Food connects us to the world. Russian philosopher Mikhail Bakhtin wrote about eating: "The body here transgresses its own limits: it swallows, devours, rends the world apart...." The food we ate in that suburban house in a small Canadian city connected us to a small village in western Ukraine and, in fact, to all the cities of Europe. But now I know how eating itself links me to ways of being in the world that are excessive, subversive, even forbidden.

My own needs and desires always felt like a burden, like a second body I carried on my back, a child who could never be fully satisfied. Food forms a bridge between the world and those desires.

Flesh of my rewritten flesh: bodies whose queer desires for food, for love, for sex, rend the world apart, and create it anew.

CHOCOLATE

Chocolate, according to Aztec legend, is a gift from the gods. The creation of the cocoa plant is attributed to the Aztec god Quetzalcoatl who, they say, descended from heaven on the beam of a star, carrying a cocoa tree pilfered from paradise. The Aztecs believed that eating the cocoa bean could furnish you with wisdom and power. Indeed, cocoa beans were so valued in parts of Central America that they were used as currency for several centuries.

I am told that when I was a very small child, I was allergic to chocolate. Strange to think of that now, since chocolate holds such currency in my adult life. But allergies can and do change over time. When I got a little older, I was able to consume chocolate in a myriad of synthetic forms, like chocolate milk sucked with a striped straw from a small, brown quarter-pint container; chocolate-glazed donuts in the school lunchroom; chocolate malts in the basement of the Hudson's Bay department store. And later, when I was older: *pain au chocolat* in Montreal, from the *patisserie* at the end of my street; Mexican chicken with chocolate *molé* sauce, eaten alone on the eve of my thirtieth birthday, in Oaxaca; and perhaps most important: Sheila's chocolate truffle cake.

Every friend of mine has their signature dish. Scrawled onto spattered index cards, handed down from ex-lovers or dead grandmothers, or long since committed to memory, these recipes are produced for birthdays, for moments of heartbreak, for potlucks, for seduction. For Penny, it's her crisp, tender roast chicken; for Megan, it's her mother's recipe for warm sundried tomato–goat cheese dip. When I visit Carolyn in Berlin, it's her strawberry-rhubarb pie I crave.

Sometimes, a person's signature dish flies in the face of who they appear to be. Often it is that person's alter ego, a representation of an inner self not easily revealed, or what the dictionary, in its secondary definition of alter ego, defines as "an intimate friend or constant companion." The blueberry pies I produce in summer are as simple and untroubled as I would like to be. My signature dish is composed of only four ingredients: butter, flour, blueberries, and sugar. The sultry tartness of the blueberries works in counterpoint to the crust's luxuriant, buttery, but straightforward presence. With this pie, what you see is what you get: no fusion, no confusion. I'd like to think that this sensual simplicity is part of me too, a secret ally that calms my inner turmoils and outer chaos.

Sheila is an old friend I met in art school two decades ago. A feminist art history scholar, she habitually lives a life of elegant austerity. The small desk on which she writes sits in a tiny, crammed living room; for the longest time, her bed was a futon on the floor. But the meals she creates are always beautiful: rich and succulent quiches, velvety *coq au vin*—they hint at a side of Sheila that may not be opulent, but insists on spiritual extravagance.

It is Sheila's chocolate truffle cake that I think of as her signature dish. She first made it for my birthday, and really, the cake is the only thing I remember from that gathering. The recipe demands eight eggs, a pound of butter, a cup of sugar, a half-cup of honey, a pound of chocolate, a cup of espresso, and no flour. Sheila's hand-written version, now taped into my recipe journal and painted with stains, is terrifyingly full of admonitions, underlinings, and exclamation marks. The melting of the chocolate must occur *slowly*. DO NOT STOP STIRRING!

A certain amount of prior scheduling is required, perhaps even the cancelling of appointments, to accommodate this cake. It takes about an hour to make, and two and a half hours to bake, at a low heat to avoid the slightly bitter taste that too many chocolate confections, baked at too high a temperature, have. The cake must then cool for at least twelve hours.

Chocolate, the romantic gift of choice for Valentine's Day, was considered an aphrodisiac by the Aztecs. Indeed, there are some 300 known chemicals in chocolate, and three in particular—caffeine, thebromine, and phenylethylamine—have a stimulating effect on the system. But Sheila's romantic culinary gestures often have an ironic undertone. One Valentine's Day in Montreal, my upstairs neighbour Ormand invited Sheila and myself to his overstuffed apartment for dinner. It so happened that all three of us were involuntarily single at the time. The plan was to drink several gin martinis, eat his oddly bland shrimp curry, complain bitterly about ex-lovers, and make disparaging comments about relationships in general. Sheila knew such an evening could only end in tears. So she brought over a chocolate layer cake festooned with our names, with hearts, and symbols of queerness—triangles and entwined women's and entwined men's symbols. It wasn't just a cake, it was a political statement. That cake transformed our bitterness. We toasted to friendship several times that night, to passionate queer friendship that, as we drunkenly affirmed, outlasts every affair and one-night stand.

In the three years that I lived in Montreal, I had many romantic liaisons, alternately good, bad, and in between. At that time, Montreal was enduring an economic depression. As a result, rents were dirt cheap and cafés and bars in the Plateau (the east side of Montreal) were always packed with unemployed *bon vivants*—myself and a stylish, insolent gang of lesbians among them. We had few obligations; most of us were unemployed and artistic, and it seemed at the time that our blood families had abandoned us. Perhaps the truth was that we had abandoned them, so that we could expand so queerly into the world.

I lived two blocks from rue Duluth, where the Bar Kiev was. On dyke night, I'd put on a tight black miniskirt, a brocade top, tights, and combat boots, throw on a leather jacket, and dash through the cold to the cavernous warmth of the bar. There was Randy, serving drinks, allowing herself a sneering smile of recognition when she saw me. Lisette and Ingrid had just started dating and were showing off, dirty dancing to "Everybody, Everybody," then heading to a bathroom stall to have sex. I had my eye on Alex, a writer who had just arrived in town from Ottawa, and she was granting me the occasional moody look in return. Most of us were from somewhere else. The emotiveness and *laissez-faire* attitude of Quebecois culture went well with a 24/7 queer lifestyle. I spent all my spare time in the bars, queer bookstores, or in dyke-run cafés. I was making up for lost time spent in repressed English Canada, and felt entitled to frequent, casual, and fabulous sex—all the time.

But the truth of the matter was that sex was never casual for me. Long after my lover of the moment had left, the imprint of her touch stayed with me for days. Most of these women only lasted a night or two in my bed, and the farewells were usually congenial. Nonetheless, I was often devastated, occasionally even heartbroken. Sheila, who lived only a few blocks from me, would come over during these bleak periods between affairs, good-naturedly bearing chocolate chip cookies or a bottle of wine.

I can't remember who my latest ex was, the time Sheila came over with a slice of her chocolate truffle cake. It must have been a significant heartbreak to have earned that particular comfort food. There must have been a weepy phone call, and vows to be celibate for the rest of my life. Sheila had family visiting at the time, so she didn't come over right away; a few days must have passed between the phone call and her visit. During that time I managed to bounce back, to give love one more chance, to throw on a little black dress and haul myself to a friend's cocktail party. There, I met a tall blonde woman named Sal. She had a liquid, laughing demeanor and, once the cocktails had run out and the last Métro train had come and gone, she went home with me. We discovered we were both femmes, not really each other's sexual type. So we cuddled and giggled and slept together rather chastely.

The next day, the doorbell tore us from our slumber at ten in the morning. I threw on Sal's shirt and ran to the door: there was Sheila, looking properly sympathetic and perhaps even apologetic, for having neglected me during my latest *crise de coeur*. She was proffering a generous slice of chocolate truffle cake, with two small separate containers of whipped cream and fruit. I managed to fabricate a heavy sigh and an anguished grimace, and accepted the cake with what I hoped looked like grace in the face of tragedy. Sheila told me she was sorry she couldn't stay, her family was waiting in the car, but she hoped I'd be all right. I told her I thought I'd probably manage for now. She gave me a quick consolatory embrace and ran back outside.

I returned immediately to my bed. I told Sal that breakfast was served; I didn't bother to get forks or plates. That cake stimulated, as it turned out, not sexual desire but a new friendship. In that sense then, the cake had the healing effect that Sheila intended.

I now live far away from Sheila's second-floor walkup on the Plateau de Montréal. I've learned how to make chocolate truffle cake myself; I've learned to enjoy love affairs that last longer than a weekend. My own recipe for desire is now not unlike Sheila's cake recipe: top quality ingredients and a long, slow baking time.

CHOCOLATE TRUFFLE CAKE

1 cup espresso coffee, brewed
½ cup honey
1 cup granulated sugar
1 lb. butter, cut into bite-sized pieces
1 lb. semi-sweet chocolate, chopped into small pieces
8 eggs, beaten

Preheat oven to 250°F. Line a 10-inch spring-form pan with tin
foil, and butter the foil. Place coffee in a double boiler, or a metal
bowl set over a pot of simmering water. Add honey and sugar, and
stir until dissolved. Add butter, stir until melted. Add chocolate
pieces; continue heating and stirring until chocolate has melted. In
a separate bowl, beat the eggs. Add a bit of the chocolate mixture
to the eggs, and stir. (Keep the rest of the chocolate mixture in the
double boiler.) Then add all of the egg mixture to the chocolate.
Continue heating, stirring constantly, until just before it starts to
thicken. When you feel it thickening on the bottom, remove from
heat. Pour into the spring-form pan and bake for 2½ hours. Remove
from oven and let cool. Store in the refrigerator at least 12 hours
before removing from the pan. Decorate with fresh fruit and serve
with whipped cream.

GRILLED SALMON

My lover Krys and I measured time in our relationship by its gustatorial highlights: the Thai noodles, fragrant with lime and cilantro, creamy with coconut milk, that I managed to produce on our first kayaking trip through Sechelt Inlet, ingredients pulled triumphantly out of a green garbage bag. The chocolate-pear torte we shared on rue Prince Arthur in Montreal, that luminous fall afternoon I first proclaimed my love. The portobello mushroom burgers with a side of mashed potatoes we'd have every week at the Templeton diner in Vancouver, our first, impassioned autumn together. Masala-spiced corn-on-the-cob we bought in India Town in Toronto, the aching, difficult week we moved in together. The perfectly grilled salmon at Citron on Queen Street West in Toronto, that tense, snowed-in winter when things between us first started to fray.

Salmon came up a lot in our relationship. It was the one thing we could count on, the one true comfort food upon which we could always agree. Ours was a spicy, tempestuous coupling, always simmering, frequently on the boil. It was as passionate as it was argumentative: the fever of attraction always did hum between us, even when we fought. Our disagreements produced a liquid heat, like the warm territories of a lake you swim into accidentally, just after the cold-water shock of plunging in. There were so many things I loved about Krys. I was aware of them even as my skin prickled with a chilly anger. And one of the things I adored the most was the fine, majestic manner with which she cooked, sparing no cost or time when money was flush, yet able to create fabulous things out of nothing when it wasn't.

The first year of the relationship was filled with romantic trips to beaches, hiking trails, and mountain vistas in Krys's beat-up but serviceable Harvest Gold 1978 VW van. Thus, a hiking trip along the Juan de Fuca Trail on the coast of Vancouver Island climaxed at Sombrio Beach with fresh salmon roasted on a beach fire overlooking the wild, open expanse of the Pacific Ocean. We didn't have a lot of fresh ingredients at hand. We combined a packet of dried dill-cucumber sauce with some yogurt and water, and basted the salmon with it. We roasted potatoes in foil, and naked corn right over the flames. We started in on a bottle of dry white British Columbia wine, sipped out of plastic coffee cups. The sun set, smoldering scarlet and orange over the roaring ocean, and we ate that hot-pink salmon redolent of woodsmoke and dill by the glow of the fire and the moon. It had a light, bitter crispiness on the outside, and inside it was tender and sweet. Afterwards, Krys stretched out on the log we were perched on and laid her head in my lap, so she could look at the stars.

By the end of our relationship, Krys and I were more efficient and prepared. We could pull together a picnic in ten minutes, and could slip in and out of an argument in about the same length of time. By then, we'd been together almost four years. Krys had come with me to Toronto for the fifteen months it took me to get a Masters degree. We had lived together then, a tender and difficult project for us both. In her awkward, halting way, she'd loved me through the deaths of my grandmother and father, which had happened within a year of each other. I stood by her through bouts of illness, and the helpless anger they churned up in her: *Why wasn't I doing more for her, why didn't I understand her?* Those days of rage were like earth tremors, making visible the faultlines in our relationship. Krys returned to British Columbia with me, this time settling outside of Vancouver, on the Sunshine Coast. The geographical distance stood in for unacknowledged fissures in the landscape of our love, tectonic plates in slow yet constant motion, heading inevitably towards a break.

For our final picnic, we packed a hibachi and a cooler of food into the van and drove to a park where Roberts Creek trickles into the ocean and where the horizon is a crooked pale blue line of mountains. My beloved was now in the habit of marinating salmon steaks in a balsamic-honey marinade and then stowing them in the freezer, in preparation for my visits. We roasted corn again, this time in foil, with the butter and salt sealed inside. Without talking much, we ate the salmon, corn, and roasted red peppers sprinkled with lemon, accompanied by a spicy California wine.

The meal was delicious; we commented on that several times. We weren't consciously aware that we were in the process of breaking up, but there was an unsettling space between our bodies, refracting each other's touch. I ran my hand down Krys's back as we sat on the beach with our blatantly illicit wine (this time we had thought to bring glass goblets), but it seemed to me that my lover's skin skimmed away from me, slippery as a bolt of silk. There were still the tender glances, welling out of the loving amber light of her hazel eyes, but there were also sharply-honed words, tasting sour in my mouth, with no contrasting sweetness to lighten the sting. And I had already been moving away from her, into spaces of intellect and spirit different from her own. Deep and complex as her love was, it had no breadth, no room for my arms and legs and spirit to swim around in, expand and grow.

The summer is fading, at the fold that always marked another year of our love. The air turns cold at night; I shiver through the fever of absence. The late afternoon light has turned to amber; the evenings are a dark purple. The apple tree in my backyard bends heavily with its load of fruit. Bereft, I have no desire to cook, but my appetite remains. The sharpness of my loss is lodged in my appetite's precision, its desire for an exact taste that will comfort, a certain exact smell that will remind me of vibrancy and life. One evening, I get chicken teriyaki takeout from my neighbourhood Japanese restaurant, its simple syrupy taste and crispy texture the exact and only combination I desire. The day after that, grilled chicken tucked into a baguette, laden with shredded vegetables and a lemony sauce, from the tiny Vietnamese café squeezed between the pawnshop and the laundromat. In between, the small random offerings of the fridge: chocolate for breakfast, blueberries for lunch. I won't have salmon for a while.

PIE

My first pie of the year is always strawberry-rhubarb.

On the west coast, eight months out of twelve are rainy, and spring appears in the subtlest gradations of green and grey. On just such a spring day, I decide to make a trip across the east side of Vancouver to Commercial Drive, a lively street of ramshackle three-storey storefronts owned by a polyglot of Italian, Portuguese, East European, and Latino merchants. I have a sensible list of errands in my back pocket; but really, this excursion is to experience the random delight of impromptu conversation with friends that "The Drive" provides: ironic chat with rock 'n' roll guitarist Elaine as we stand in the drugstore; sly, queer repartee with Laiwan, a fellow artist, outside WaaZubee's Café. It's to feed my senses, which have been starved of primary colours and flowery smells: the impossible scarlet of local hothouse peppers; the blush on the skin of a blood orange; the delicate pink and red of the rhubarb.

That evening, three friends come to dinner: the asparagus with blood orange sauce elicits applause. It is one of the simpler recipes from a cookbook called *The Girls Who Dish!*, written collaboratively by Vancouver's best women chefs. Melt a teaspoon of butter, stir in some finely chopped shallot, and then, a minute later, the juice of two blood oranges and one teaspoon of lemon juice. Removing it from the heat, swirl in more butter, a fistful of chopped fresh thyme; salt and pepper to taste. Pour it over lightly steamed asparagus, sprinkling orange zest over top.

The pie I make for dessert features the sweet-and-sour duet of strawberry and rhubarb and the gentle crunch of streusel topping, melty vanilla ice cream on the side.

My second pie of the year is accidental. It is June. Lemon-coloured light serrates the dark green shadows of my garden. The last of the Icelandic poppies nod in the breeze; the first red cherries from a neighbour's tree fall softly to the ground. Apricots have appeared at Garway, the Asian grocery near my house, and raspberries at another shop down the road. The colours and textures are irresistible, so I buy both. Pale orange quadrants of apricots mix with raspberries in a glass bowl on my blue-tiled kitchen counter. For my pie, I lace the opposing flavours together with maple syrup and a touch of fresh grated ginger.

The crust is a *Joy of Cooking* classic. Now, a word here must be said about this much-maligned cookbook's respect for pie. A full three pages (of my mother's spattered, well-worn 1953 edition, that is) are devoted to a preamble regarding the finer points of pastry—after which one can find recipes for over forty pies. (Even more impressive for these times, the 1997 edition's pie preamble has expanded to over ten pages.) There is a time chart for baking, advice on pans, some nifty diagrams related to issues of rolling, fluting, and latticing, and a haiku of terse final hints:

1. *Too much flour makes pie crust tough.*
2. *Too much shortening makes it dry and crumbly.*
3. *Too much liquid makes it heavy and soggy.*

The Joy of Cooking's authors Irma S. Rombauer and Marion Rombauer Becker are not above inserting some tart admonitions ("If a pie is to have a deep filling, and to me this is the ideal pie, a deep pie pan will be a great help"). But generally, this is valuable pie-maker's lore: a compendium of lost wisdom. New tins will *not* produce a nicely browned bottom crust. Keep the moisture *out* and the air *in*. If feasible, chill the dough for *twelve hours*. If the filling will be juicy, brush the bottom crust with egg white or melted butter so it *won't* get soggy. Brush the top with milk, and it will be glossy once baked. Two pieces of macaroni, placed in the top crust like vents, will keep juices from boiling over.

The beauty of pie is in its making. These days, in a departure from family tradition, I have eschewed packaged Tender Flake shortening for the poetic luxury of *pâté brisée*. I measure two cups of flour into a large bowl, then a teaspoon of salt. In goes a half-pound of cold butter, which I break up with a knife. Two knives, a pastry blender or, luxury of luxuries, a food processor, serve to integrate the butter with the flour until it has the texture of cornmeal. A quarter cup or more of ice water help to bind the dough together as I blend it quickly with my hands. I form it into two balls, rolling each one out separately between two pieces of wax paper. I place the bottom crust into the pan, a round white sheet, smooth and pliable as unbleached cotton. Then I pour in the filling and cover it with the reserved circle of dough, which has been chilling in the fridge. Bake the pie for anywhere between forty-five minutes to an hour, or until filling starts to bubble out from the slits in the crust.

I love the look of pie at this point, the handcraftedness of it, the aesthetics of symmetrically placed slits, the fluted, sealed crust. The way I know how to make pastry links me, over time and space, to the ways of my mother and grandmother: the sway of my body as I roll the dough; the movement of my hands as I pat and patch the dough into the pan.

The third pie of the year is blackberry. This pie is usually made during an annual end-of-summer visit to friends, Glen and Jeanette, who live in the tiny community of Fanny Bay, on the east coast of Vancouver Island.

The martini glasses are chilling by the time I arrive on their doorstep in late afternoon. I have taken a cab, a bus, a ferry, and finally a minivan shuttle to get to their place. The last long, flat rays of sun bleach the outlines of faraway islands to pale blue. We nibble on cold local sockeye salmon, crackers, and artisan cheese from the Comox Valley. Glen fills me in on the opening of a Wal-Mart store in a nearby town. Wal-Mart, the wealthiest corporation in North America, is infamous for its labour-busting practices, its music censorship, and its destruction of small businesses. Glen, a filmmaker, has been documenting various protests and city hall meetings. Jeanette, trained in herbology, gives me advice on remedies for my mother, who's been battling cancer, and suddenly the kitchen table is full of her reference books, the air full of her sweet concern. Glen quietly starts preparing fried Fanny Bay oysters, as he always does when I visit.

I can't get enough of those oysters. They are salty and sweet in exactly the right proportions. They are voluptuous. They have attitude and style. At the right time of day and the right time of year, you can gather them yourself. You don't even have to shuck them: simply roast them on a campfire or over a barbecue grill, and they will open up. A squirt of lemon and they're ready to eat, with a smoky flavour all their own.

Glen uses the recipe that they hand out at the fish store at Buckley Bay. Jeanette has me gather lettuce, arugula, tomatoes, green onions, peas, and dill from her garden edged with sunflowers. When I return to the kitchen, Jeanette hands me a second martini and gets right to the point.

"So. What's happening with you and Krys?"

"Oh. We broke up. I totally forgot to tell you."

Jeanette, silent for a moment, bites her lip. Glen, hard at

work breading the oysters, laughs out loud. Jeanette silences him with a well-aimed glare.

"Oh. OK. Well, that's too bad. How are you feeling?"

I can tell Jeanette is trying to hide her disappointment. She loves Krys and her hippie-ish, outdoorsy ways. I think she imagined us all kayaking together into the sunset, two by two, like Noah's ark.

"I'm fantastic. How are you?"

Jeanette sighs, and puts some water on to boil for the green beans.

"Anyways, I'm seeing someone new. TJ."

"That's my girl!" Glen blurts out. He walks over to Jeanette and feeds her a morsel of salmon.

"Oh, good," Jeanette replies, unconvincingly. "What's she like?" And then, ready to open up her heart again, she asks, hopefully, "Does she like kayaking?"

I tell them about TJ's PhD in critical theory and her great talent for mixing martinis. I rhapsodize about her intellect, our sexual attraction, the great road trips we're going to have. I fail to mention her intense dislike of any form of transportation not involving her Audi. Jeanette says all the right things, then wipes away a quick tear. Breakups, it seems, can be as hard on the friends as they are on the lovers themselves.

The only way to resolve the situation is to make pie. The next morning, while my hosts are still sleeping, I go out to pick berries. As I cut across the beach, dragonflies cast shadows on the sand, making a sound like miniature outboard motors. Crows squawk from the bushes. Torn-paper strips of clouds float across the mountaintops. There's a premonition of autumn in the early morning air.

The berries, already warm to the touch, fall easily from their branches. By the time I get back to the house, Glen is firing up the woodstove, then cranks up bluegrass music on the CD player. I set about making blackberry pie. We eat it while still warm after a lunch of vegetable soup. It's raining gently; a chill is settling in.

It seems all is forgiven. The lazy afternoon draws to a close, and the clouds blow away. We go for a dusky swim as the water wearies of its early evening peach hue, decides to dress up for the evening and turns suddenly, and dramatically, to gold.

CARROT CAKE

I was in love again. An elaborate courtship with TJ filled my weekends with beach picnics and urban culinary adventures. We cooed and held hands over poached eggs with sautéed chanterelle mushrooms; argued queer theory over wasabi-encrusted prawns; lay on the beach reading the Sunday *New York Times* and sharing a sour cherry Danish. My new love and I ate and talked about food constantly: the fresh oysters, prawns, and wine we needed to buy for dinner, how much we adored the tapas at a local Spanish restaurant, and whether to make a tomato or a cream sauce for the next day's manicotti.

It had been almost a year since my breakup with Krys when TJ and I got together. I was completing the final, dreary requirements of my doctorate. My mind felt dry as a bone; my soul felt like it had shrunk somehow. TJ's elaborate attentions were a gift out of nowhere. I ignored all the storm warnings—impatient nature, swift judgments, a breathtaking arrogance—and fell head over heels in love. It was a dangerous, hungry sort of love.

Hunger doesn't always have to do with food. Some days I'm hungry for attention or some kind of instant, fast food love: from friends, students, co-workers. I can trace that hunger like a road, through life's unwieldy twists and turns, all the way back to childhood. TJ's less charming characteristics, as familiar as the names of all my siblings or the litany of my father's wartime traumas, dangerously secured my devotion to her. She provoked a deep femininity in me, as well as a culinary courage I never knew I had. I cooked for her as I had never cooked before: Spanish appetizers, Thai curries, and Italian tortas landed before her in dizzying, delectable profusion. Without realizing it, I was connecting back to a lost territory: the place where two rivers met, my femininity and my ethnicity. Powerful and deadly; sweet and sour.

TJ's birthday was coming up, and I decided to bake her a cake. I'm not really much of a baker, and what's more, she lived a ferry ride away in Victoria. I knew I'd have to package it somehow, because she lived in one city and I in another. I'd have to carry it into a taxi, then onto a bus, a ferry, and finally, a car. Not to mention the fact that my mother was visiting me again, and she might not approve.

My mother seemed tired when she arrived in Vancouver, and a little bit sad, but she was alive and she knew it. Her body told the story of her surgery and her recovery; yet despite her fatigue, her eyes were sharp and clear. Wherever we went that visit she noticed everything, all the details: who was poor, who was rich, the racial breakdown of the crowds at the public market, the fine distinctions between the pâtés we tasted at one booth, the quality of the fish at another.

When we weren't shopping or sightseeing, my mother commandeered the couch, captain of a battleship. Kleenex, medicines, and food magazines covered the coffee table. She kept one eye on the TV, the other on me, her "unmarried" daughter. I could tell what she was thinking: *what a strange girl, what an odd one.* I made up a bed with fresh, sweet-smelling sheets for her, cooked beautiful, smooth soups, bought salmon mousse and goat cheese, rented a pile of videos. Perhaps my mother felt that all my skills at homemaking were wasted, with no husband or kids to love and care for. It seemed to make no sense to her that she herself was the beneficiary, the dear one, an inheritance flowing upriver from daughter to mother, instead of the other way around.

"I'm going to bake TJ a birthday cake," I said to my mother, right after a story on same-sex marriage on the six o'clock news. She said nothing, instead exhaling a chill silence that expanded like vapour and lingered until *Oprah* the next day. She hadn't taken to TJ, whom I'd smuggled in, uninvited, to Christmas Eve dinner the year before. I put a video into the VCR: *As Good as It Gets*, with Jack Nicholson as Melvin, an obsessive-compulsive writer, and Helen Hunt as Carol, the only waitress in New York who will put up with him. I got flour, sugar, oil, and eggs out of the cupboard and set myself to grating carrots, buttering and flouring a spring-form pan. "I need a compliment, and I need it now," I heard Carol say after Melvin insulted her on their first date. "You make me want to be a better man," replied Melvin, grudgingly, sweetly.

I sat down with my mom to watch my favourite parts: Carol, Melvin, and Simon, a gay man Jack had reluctantly taken under his wing, were on a road trip to Simon's hometown. Strange alliances and hostilities arose. I watched my mom surreptitiously: she smiled broadly, then shook her head and tsk-tsked when things got bad between Carol and Melvin.

I returned to the cake: it was more work than I'd bargained for, with its little extras like pineapple and coconut. I was unsure about the state of my baking powder or whether I should add an extra egg, the batter seemed so stiff. In the movie, Simon called his parents when the three of them got to his hometown, but they wouldn't pick up the phone, they were that homophobic. He was bitter, but not for long. He and Carol spent a chaste night together. Melvin got jealous. I put the cake in the oven, and soon the sweet smell of baking filled my apartment.

When they returned from their road trip, Carol told

Melvin, "I never want to see you again." Ten minutes later, they were kissing on the street under a lamppost on a sultry New York night. Credits rolled. I pulled the cake out of the oven, and I made my mother get up and have a look at it. She sniffed it gingerly, and poked it. "Yes," she said with reluctant approval, "it's good."

The next day, I escorted my mother to the airport bus and then hopped into a cab. The cake travelled with me in a shopping bag from Vancouver to Victoria. At the last minute, I made cream cheese icing, unbearably rich, sprinkled with chopped walnuts. I put thirty-six candles on the cake, and TJ blew out the candles as heat and embarrassment and pleasure flushed her cheeks. It was a kind of performance piece, that cake: screwball comedy meets domestic bliss. It was the only birthday of hers we'd ever celebrate together. Still, the cake was perfect, moist and sweet with pineapple, coconut, and carrot, and the distance love had to travel, giving it an edge.

CARROT CAKE WITH CREAM CHEESE ICING

2 cups all-purpose flour
2 cups granulated sugar
2 tsp cinnamon
1 tsp nutmeg
1½ tsp baking soda
2 tsp vanilla extract
½ tsp salt
1 ½ cups vegetable oil
3 eggs, beaten
1 cup coconut, shredded
2 cups carrots, finely grated (about 4 carrots)
1 8-oz can crushed pineapple, well-drained
1 cup walnuts or pecans, chopped (optional)

Preheat oven to 350°F. In a large bowl, combine the first 7 ingredients, and stir to blend. Add eggs, oil, carrots, and vanilla; beat until well blended. Stir in pineapple, coconut, and ½ cup of the nuts. Pour into a greased, floured 9"x13" pan. Bake for 50 to 60 minutes, or until a toothpick inserted in centre comes out clean. Use remaining nuts to press into icing (see below). This cake keeps moist and is good for about a week.

ICING:
¼ cup butter, softened
4 oz cream cheese, softened
1 cup icing sugar
1 tsp vanilla extract
Combine butter and cream cheese; cream until light and fluffy. Add sugar and vanilla, mixing well. Let cake cool completely before icing.

ORANGES

Scent of orange, floating loosely over a lover's skin. Scent of orange at Christmas time, wooden box of mandarins cracked open, layer of purple tissue unpeeled, skin open to flesh, flesh open to mouth.

Oranges may not be the only fruit, but as far as I am concerned, they are the most sensual. They hold a secret illicit charge for me, despite their wholesome reputation. Orange juice, is, of course, the sacred drink of North American breakfasts. It was orange juice maven Anita Bryant, after all, who led a campaign against homosexuals in Florida in the 1970s. Orange for family, orange for normalcy.

Nothing normal about it.

At Penny's Passover meal, there is a single orange on the table, next to the lamb shank, the *charoset*, and the roasted egg. We read the feminist Haggadah she wrote, which quotes an angry man (coincidentally, from Florida, the land of oranges) saying to a feminist rabbi, "A woman belongs on the pulpit as much as an orange belongs on the Seder plate!" The orange, argues this revisionist Haggadah, "belongs there as a symbol that women belong wherever Jews carry on a sacred life."

The combination of orange and chocolate evokes Christmas for me, which is to say, my version of Christmas. Blood family and chosen family, orange and chocolate, tart and sweet. A taste on my tongue like something unexpected, like that rare combination of family, lover, and friends I have been searching for all my life.

Last Christmas, the rain poured and poured, and the Vancouver air delivered its curious autumnal aroma of leaf mold and cedar. People were counting how many days it had been raining, a bad sign: Zoë claimed it had been sixty-seven days and four hours since we'd last seen the sun. It was almost a month since TJ had left me, and exactly a year since she and I had spent a romantic week on Galiano Island. It was eighty-four days since she'd told me she wanted to be with me forever. That December, I said to my friends, I am *so* not going to participate in all the Christmas hoopla—but then off I went to the Drive to buy pannetone from Emilio, the baker with the sad dark eyes, and I ate it every morning that month, toasted and then slathered with butter. That December, I watched too much TV, blue waves of Christmas specials and ads keeping me down at the bottom of a thought-free ocean.

On one such December afternoon, the rain stopped for a few hours, and a tarnished yellow light glimmered through my French doors. That was also the day Penny and Kim decided that what I needed most in life was a Christmas tree. They picked me up in Kim's 4x4 and drove me against my will to the Produce City parking lot, where a man with a flashy grin showed us his "winter collection." Penny and Kim spent the better part of an hour hotly discussing the merits of Scotch pine versus Douglas fir. Kim was insistent on a particularly bushy tree that, to my mind, looked far too large for my low-ceilinged apartment. But with some minor trimming, the tree co-operated, and its branches fanned out gracefully in my apartment, blocking what little winter light was left. We decorated it with the tacky assortment of ornaments I'd gathered over the years: homemade painted walnut shells; orange slices preserved with varnish. Getting into the mood, I served them good Dutch hot chocolate, tiny goblets of orange liqueur on the side. I put on the corny Ukrainian Christmas CD I always play over and over, the one where Roman's bandura music glimmers in the background. Penny and Kim tolerated this with good humour and exasperation. They could see their medicine had taken.

A few days later, I would head to Edmonton to be with my other family, the haphazard grouping of individuals also known as my blood relations. Hurriedly booking a plane ticket, I forgot everything I knew about family at Christmas time: judgments and misjudgments, and a cornucopia of isms; the damp, uneasy comfort of it all.

When I got to my mother's house, she kissed me lightly on both cheeks, trying to hide her relief that I had come. She immediately served me a plate of perogies with sour cream, even though it was well past suppertime. Out of the corner of my eye, I noticed a wooden bowl of mandarin oranges on the coffee table.

On Christmas Eve, we ate the traditional foods: cabbage rolls, mushroom sauce, borscht, and heaps of perogies. My uncle decried the mixing of races, my sister-in-law described her family's summer vacation in a small mountain town in horrifying detail, and I contemplated escaping by cab to a gay bar in a seedy part of town. My sister Jeannie's crimson face overflowed with everything it usually tries to hide. Little Sonya, her daughter, gave her a warning look. Chrissy carefully swerved her eyes towards and away from this scene with practiced cool. Natalie, seated next to me, ignored the drama and asked me what had happened with TJ. I swallowed back the whole story and muttered simply, "She's toast." My mother sat with frail authority at the head of the table, where my father used to preside. We joked, as usual, about that morbid Ukrainian Christmas tradition of setting a place at the table for the dead. We did not do so, claiming there were not enough forks or knives, or table space, to spare. Our dead were with us nonetheless, making their presence known in small silences, and in my mother's face, caught unawares, in the careful space between sorrow and celebration.

That January, I relocated to Toronto. I had completed my PhD. I needed to get away from that low-ceilinged apartment, needed to give myself a physical sense of having moved on.

A year passed, full of speeded-up film frames: a blur of work and renewed friendships, of hurrying back and forth across a large, unruly city in streetcars whose windows revealed overly bright colours of possibility. Christmas appeared once again on the horizon. I searched the city for oranges: Japanese oranges, we used to call them. My Baba always had a box or two on hand; the oranges were usually wrapped in purple tissue and they were always succulent and honey-sweet. I went to Kensington Market; to my corner store on Dundas Street; to the No Frills supermarket in at Dufferin Mall. I bought only a few at a time, experimenting: oranges from Morocco, from China, from California. One varietal was too sour, the other too seedy; yet another was dry and pulpy. Finally, I pretty much gave up on oranges, and bought a small bottle of Grand Marnier to pour into my hot chocolate, as a substitute for that round, plump flavour.

One evening, at Terri and Cap's pre-Christmas turkey dinner, which they host early in the season for all their queer friends, I hit the bullseye. Over conversation with Gisele, an aspiring organic farmer, I absently took an orange from a bowl. As we talked, I peeled it and tasted a morsel. Full, sweet-sour flavour bloomed on my tongue. I ate another piece, just to make sure, and then asked wonderingly of my hosts where these oranges were from. "Loblaws," said Cap, and she showed me the box, a faux wooden half-crate with a logo that beared the name *Stephanie*, which made me think of a pleasant, plump, do-gooder girl. "Oh, Loblaws," I repeated wistfully. The closest Loblaws was a bus and a subway ride from my home. It was only a week before Christmas; I'd never have time to go there. We moved onto other topics of conversation as Terri served up her homemade shortbread, which was exquisite. I forgot all about those perfect oranges.

The next day, I came home quite late. Winter had finally slammed the city, and my face felt dry and stiff, like I'd had a home facial and left the oatmeal mask on too long. It was December sixth: for some reason, I remembered that this was St Nicholas Day, the traditional time of gift-giving in Eastern European cultures. Indeed, on this day, we were often given oranges. The thought of this made me feel like crap as I clambered awkwardly across a snowdrift to get to my front door and into my dark, lonely apartment.

Something on the porch caught my eye. A small box—probably something belonging to my upstairs neighbour, I thought. Then I noticed the pretty blue logo in a serif font: *Stephanie*. There she was again, that sweet, self-effacing girl. Right there on the porch, I dialed up Terri's number on my cell phone to thank her and Cap. "No, no, it wasn't us," said Terri, mysteriously. "Well, then, who the hell was it?" I asked. "I can't tell you," said Terri self-importantly, savouring my confusion. "They asked me not to say. They said to tell you it's from a secret angel."

I entered my apartment. My cat came to the door to greet me, sniffing the Stephanie box suspiciously. I stood for a moment in the middle of my kitchen, in the middle of a huge, anonymous, snow-bound city, my coat still on. I had vertigo at the thought of someone performing this very specific yet random act of kindness just for me. I put the oranges in a wooden bowl and then I peeled one open, savouring its perfume.

RECIPE FOR TROUBLE

"You're so feminine," whispered Lila, my new girlfriend, as I flipped impatiently through my recipe files, trying to find asparagus risotto. She shivered with delight as she said it, and touched my face with her smooth-as-kid-leather hand. I was dressed that day in jeans and a hoodie, no earrings, no lipstick. I felt like she could see inside of me and I didn't know what she saw. But I liked it: I felt recognized.

How does an identity so deeply felt get formed? Did I learn it in my Baba and Mama's kitchen, along with the best way to make strudel and the quickest way to preserve pickles?

In principle at least, I picked up my culinary skills from my mother. Mama is a consummate intuitive cook, the pinch-of-this and splash-of-that kind. She's a one-woman show in the kitchen, definitely not an ensemble player. If my sisters and I were asked to help, it was strictly supporting actress stuff: washing greasy pots or lugging mysterious foil-wrapped items up from the freezer in the basement. Even now, when my mother visits and offers to show me how to make something—her perogies, her borscht—the exact details of technique, like kneading or braising, are difficult to master, because my mother will not readily allow for collaboration. She enters into a kind of trance while she's cooking, and her movements are all femme poetry: rhythmic, graceful, refined to necessity.

It is by watching and tasting that I learn from my mother. The passionate bend and thrust of her body as she's rolling dough; the delicate, mincing gestures of filling it; the call and response of tasting and seasoning a broth. "What do you think?" she asks anxiously, solicitously, feeding me a table-spoon of soup. "More salt?" ... "It needs a little something" ... "That stock isn't quite right...." Flavouring takes time and much consideration. Spontaneity, too: a sudden, impetuous squeeze of lemon into the chicken soup; the last-minute extravagance of herbed garlic croutons for the gazpacho. My mother's dishes always have a perfect blend of high and low notes, as in her borscht: the daintiness of dill overlaid onto the robust *profundo* of beef stock and beetroot, a sensual dollop of sour cream their coda.

Femme is related to feminine, but it's not the same thing. It's a distillation, like a pan of balsamic vinegar that's been reduced to a sweet, elegant sauce. Femininity with a twist, with attitude. My mother who, even now in her seventies, charms the shopkeepers and then bargains them down to a price they hadn't considered. My friend Terri with her shoulder-length bleached blonde hair, her demure outfits, her potty mouth when you piss her off.

A butch enters my house for the first time, offering me a bottle of wine with boyish awkwardness. She notices there are candles everywhere and a mess of vegetables, bottles, and pots on the kitchen counter. I take my future lover by the hand, lead her to the kitchen, give her a glass of wine, place a plate of cheeses and sliced baguette between us. And then I cook while my future lover watches me covertly: I swish the sauce-pan over the flame, tossing in slivers of shallots, deglazing with wine. I serve the food finally and my lover's eyes and body meet mine.

It's about bodies in the end, and the ways in which they recognize each other. Lila, with her boyish ways, needed me to be a girly girl, and sometimes, as I changed into a dress and served her a fragrant plate of steaming risotto, that's what I let her have. She and I both knew what a bittersweet, uneasy reci-pe for trouble this was: ancestral tradition mixed with queer.

Lila looked to me like a boy sometimes, like a woman at others. I saw the masculinity that was so deep and true and painful in her, that was different from being a man.

My Baba never cooked risotto, wouldn't have ever known what it was. But I serve food for my lovers the same way she did. Always, an excess of food, it's rude to make only enough. Always, an eye on the beloved's dish—"Here, have some more," and, before you know it, just like my Baba, I've cunningly refilled my lover's plate. Trust me, my butch lovers never go away hungry.

It took me a long time to figure it out: that's what feeds the hunger inside of me.

ASPARAGUS LEMON RISOTTO

4 tbsp unsalted butter
¼ cup shallots, finely chopped
1½ cups arborio rice
1 cup wild mushrooms, sliced
4 tsp roasted garlic (about 1 roasted head)
½ cup dry white wine or dry vermouth
5-6 cups heated vegetable or chicken stock
½ cup Parmesan, Romano or Asiago cheese, freshly grated
2 tsp lemon zest
¾ cup asparagus, diagonally sliced into ½-inch pieces
Salt and pepper to taste

In a saucepan over medium heat, melt 3 tbsp of butter. Add shallots and sauté until soft. Stir in rice and mushrooms and cook, stirring constantly until rice is translucent, about 10 minutes. Add garlic, wine or vermouth, and ½ cup of the hot stock. Cook, stirring constantly, until liquid is absorbed. Continue adding small amounts of stock in this manner, stirring all the while, until rice is creamy but firm, about 20 to 30 minutes. When done, stir in remaining butter, cheese, lemon zest, and asparagus. Season to taste with salt and pepper. Makes 4 servings.

COMFORT FOOD FOR BREAKUPS

By my mid-thirties, I had experienced love in all its forms—sweet, nasty, pedestrian, intelligent, tawdry, sophisticated. I was grateful for all of it. I had finally left the suburbs and all the hand-me-down traumas of war and immigration, or so it seemed. I was learning new words, like "lover" and "love-life": phrases unspeakably glamorous, like champagne sparkling in my throat. I became devoted to pleasure, a term I didn't even know the word for in my mother tongue. And alas, I became experienced at breakups.

Queers of my generation have a lot to say about breakups. We could write a book. We've fallen in and out of love more often than most. We had to learn about love through primary research—no romantic queer feature films or quirky gay-themed sitcoms to show us how. Our first loves were so tentative, so full of doubt. We were inventors, we were social scientists, coming up with completely new forms of pain and betrayal.

My first lesbian breakup was a huge mess. It occurred in a large, shabby communal house in the west end of Toronto. My lover, Janey, a nervous, pretty, femmy temp worker, left a message on the answering machine to tell me it was over. The fact that she could just as easily have told me in person, since we lived together in the same lesbian-feminist-vegetarian co-op, didn't seem funny at the time. There were five women in the co-op, and everyone felt obliged to take sides. Needing, for obvious reasons, to get out of there, I went for a long walk. I ended up on Dundas Street, at a Portuguese churrascaria. *Churrasco* means barbecue; chicken prepared this way is one of the best comfort foods for breakups there is. It's slathered with piri-piri, a hot red chili sauce, and either roasted on a spit or grilled over a fire. It's salty and sweet at the same time, and the chicken is tender, delicious. With my half-chicken I also ordered the curiously-named "Parisienne potatoes," perfectly shaped melon balls of greasy roasted spuds. I took my bulging Styrofoam container to Trinity-Bellwoods Park and had a triumphant, solitary meal. I had lost my queer virginity, I had learned a few moves, and, like the Gloria Gaynor song that was playing in all the clubs at the time, I would survive.

Not all breakups end with such culinary satisfaction. I was soon to discover that some relationships go deep, deeper than skin, and that my skin was porous and absorbed too much. I told myself that each relationship was like a new layer of skin building upon the last, making me stronger, wiser, more able to love. But perhaps there is a moment, a certain fulcrum in one's life, when the scales begin to tip the other way. Skin contracts after it expands. Scar tissue appears.

Over the years, I experienced all manner of breakup, from friendly and nonchalant to excruciatingly drawn out. One friend of mine likened a lesbian breakup to a car going downhill with the brakes on. The decade passed and the inventory of breakup stories grew. I could have written a book. I did.

For all of the affairs and dates I'd had by the time I reached my thirties, Mona was really my first passionate love, and I still can't explain why. She worked in a bookstore, and was geeky before geeky was in. She wore baggy clothes, most of them denim, at least five years out of date. Her glasses were huge on her sallow, small-boned face, and her eyes, alarmingly magnified behind them, were cartoon-wide. She lived hundreds of miles away, in a small city I disliked, and stuttered unattractively over the phone. But after our first, ill-conceived liaison in a friend's apartment in Toronto, I had an unquenchable thirst for the feel of her skin against mine.

Mona, who felt, she said, so *amateur* next to me, was a quick learner, a serious student of my body's pleasure. She memorized its various zones and knew the statistical variation of touch between one place and another. She read my body like it was the only, the best, the most important book in the world. But when she put her glasses back on and stared at me in deer-caught-in-headlights bewilderment, I'd go, *OK, whatever, this can't continue.* And then, with one shaky, tentative touch from her, I was back in that wet, slippery, hungry, thirsty, and impossibly satisfying realm. I resigned myself to acid-washed denim. I thought seriously about moving to the unpleasant central Ontario city.

A harsh and painful breakup was in the cards, as surely as night follows day. The details are unimportant. It happened two years after we met, in the spring, and I didn't recover until the following winter. I lost my appetite, ate only enough to keep my blood sugar at tolerable levels. I lost twenty pounds. I moved to Vancouver. A friend placed a homemade meal in front of me, I think it was lamb moussaka, and I began to eat again.

After that, my loving slowed down, matured.

My last breakup was not such a great tragedy—a fling that ran into logistical problems, seeing as I was leaving town for the summer. Lila was a special one, and slightly eccentric, too. She had a soulful dark gaze, the trauma of migration like blood in her eyes. She had a wide, brilliant smile and an arrogant way of carrying her small stature that I found lovable. She wore khaki work shirts and men's baggy wool pants; underneath those were Calvin Klein boxer shorts. We'd shared some of the coincidences of eastern cultures linked by the Silk Road: a fanatical belief in hospitality and the profound importance of sharing a meal.

Like my grandmother, Lila wasn't merely interested in food: she worried constantly about it. Worried I wasn't eating enough, worried we'd offend the cook in a restaurant if we left any food on our plates. She was worried about the *ghormeh sabzi* (green herb stew) she'd bring to her mother the next day, worried she wouldn't like it. She was the youngest daughter in her family; it fell to her to take care of her parents, old and frail as they were. Sometimes, it hurt me to look into her sad brown eyes, I saw so much of my history there.

I liked to cook for Lila, make her feel cared for. She sighed with pleasure when I served her the simplest of meals: cheese omelette; lentil soup; salad greens with a vinaigrette dressing. It was so much like family. But food was also where the trouble began. One day, Lila invited me to her house for a meal. "I've filled the fridge with food," she said, in a phone message, knowing that would charm me. I phoned her back and accepted the invitation. Coyly, jokingly, I asked, "If I stay overnight, will you make me breakfast, too?" She hung up the phone. I didn't hear from her for a week. She finally revealed to me in injured tones that in her culture it was the highest offence to *ask* for food. It implied some possible oversight on the part of the host, an unimaginable insult. To make amends, I invited her over for homemade strawberry-rhubarb pie. She accepted, then bailed at the last minute, even though I had spent an entire spring morning labouring over the crust.

And so it went, for weeks on end. One day when I was sick, Lila left a message on my voicemail: "Sweetie, I made you chicken soup. You're gonna love it: free-range chicken breasts, tarragon, egg noodles, yum. It's in my trunk, I can drop it by whenever you feel like it."

I phoned her back, sleepy and feverish, and left a message saying, "Sure, but only if it's no trouble."

The soup never made it to my house; I'd been too hesitant in my reply. Then there was a batch of oatmeal-coconut-chocolate chip cookies I made for her but couldn't bring myself to deliver, she'd been so rude. There was always some delectable food item between us, proffered, refused, denied, uneaten. It was so terribly familiar: food as reward, food as punishment, food sizzling with anger or perfumed with love. I felt ashamed at all the wasted effort, the disappointments. I was dismayed by all the spoiled food. It couldn't continue.

After our breakup, I spent a week floating in the TV's oceanic glow, remote in hand. I watched *Like Water for Chocolate*, a film about a Mexican family whose youngest daughter, Tita, has been forbidden by her mother to marry the man she loves. According to tradition, she must care for her Mama Elena until she dies. Tita pours all of her passion, love, and bitterness into her cooking, affecting everyone in the family. And finally, that's how she gets her revenge, too—through food.

I wept throughout that film, and for the rest of the week. It was as though every breakup, every sad farewell had gotten mixed into our parting of ways. I subsisted for days on canned tuna, saltine crackers, and pears.

After ten days, I suddenly felt incredibly hungry. I pored through my cupboards. Amid the cracker boxes and cans of beans I found a small red tin, with cookies inside, wrapped in wax paper, and a note: *For L, the ultimate comfort food, love, M*. I poured myself a glass of cheap Scotch, put on a Gloria Gaynor CD I'd purchased recently at a yard sale and ate the whole tin of chocolate chip oatmeal cookies myself.
Oh no, not I. I would survive.

CHOCOLATE CHIP OATMEAL COOKIES

I cup butter
1 cup brown sugar, lightly packed
1 tsp baking soda
½ cup boiling water
1 tsp vanilla extract
1 egg, beaten
1¾ cups flour
½ tsp salt
2 cups quick oats
½ cup dried coconut
1 cup semi-sweet chocolate chips

Preheat oven to 350°F. In a bowl, cream the butter, then blend
in the sugar until well mixed. Dissolve the baking soda in boiling
water and add it to the butter-sugar mixture, followed by the vanilla
and the egg. In another bowl, stir together the flour, salt, oats, and
coconut, then add them slowly to the creamed mixture. Mix well.
Stir in the chocolate chips. Form small balls, place on a greased
cookie sheet, flatten with a fork, and bake for 12 to 15 minutes. You
can also freeze all or part of this batter and use, defrosted, when
desired. Makes about 30 cookies.

VARENNYKY

You may not be familiar with *varennyky*.

It's a food item but also a word, with its own history of colonization. No one knows the exact origin of *varennyky*, those delectable, excessive buttery dumplings stuffed with potato and cheese. Some say their similarity to Chinese potstickers indicates the influence of invading Mongols and Tatars. But the word *varennyk* itself—meaning, small cooked thing—is Ukrainian. *Perohy*, the more commonly used term, is Polish, and originates from the word *pirog*, which means pie. Coming from Western Ukraine, long colonized by Poland, my parents had many vernacular Polish-isms in their speech. So, *perohy* it was. But as we got older my overly-patriotic father decided that some of our ways of being Ukrainian weren't Ukrainian enough. Suddenly and tragically, Christmas got switched from December 25 to January 6 (a trauma from which I still haven't fully recovered). And, *perohy* became *varennyky*.

Whatever the shift in terminology, the taste and feel of my mother's *varennyky* has never changed: rich, silky smooth, with a bit of bite on the outside, and soft and pillowy, with a bit of texture, on the inside. I have never tried to estimate the amount of calories and fat contained in one *varennyk*, but let's just say that those who fear a heart attack need not apply. The effect of so much butter in one serving can, I have found, produce dizziness and euphoria in those unaccustomed to such excess in a savoury dish.

Once, after bringing some of my mother's freshly-made *varennyky* to a dinner party, my deliriously sated hosts staggered from the table, drunk on carbs and fat. They insisted on phoning my mother to express their gratitude, and so they did, passing the phone to one another and slathering on the superlatives. Much later, my mother, commenting on this unusual phone call, asked me, in helpless bewilderment: *Were they joking?*

Varennyky are, to my mother's mind, nothing special: something you always have on hand, like bread and milk. Once you have mastered the fine art of dough-making, the exact proportion of ingredients (none of which have been precisely recorded), the delicate gestures of mixing, and the complex technologies of kneading, cutting, stuffing, sealing, boiling, serving, and storing—a skill set which could take thirty years to perfect—there's really nothing to it.

I do not attempt *varennyky*. There are far too many variables, I don't have the nerve to use so much butter, and they'll never be as good as my mother's. Nonetheless, I respect the iconic value of *varennyky*, and the sense of ritual that accrues to them. Because it's actually quite boring to make 100 circles of dough stuffed with potato and cheese, my mother will often get together with her women friends—those tempestuous ladies also known as the Divas of the Church—and they will make *varennyky* together. No doubt these sessions are accompanied by the deeply pleasurable telling of tragic family stories, not to mention naughty gossip about other ladies and other families. Delicate sips of brandy or peach schnapps may lubricate the conversation. There's a kind of peasant ethos to these perogy work parties: it's wrong to just sit around and have fun. It's better to combine celebration with work, and to do it with others.

The last time my mother asked me to help make *varennyky*, I reluctantly complied. We'd had a disagreement earlier, and I wanted to make amends. I poured myself a glass of a good shiraz and defiantly sat down at the kitchen table (my mother always stands). I opened up the Sunday *New York Times* and read the book review section while stuffing the dough and pinching it shut. I found this to be quite a satisfactory arrangement; my mother thought this very odd, but quite funny, too. It's a story she enjoys telling to others, some kind of snapshot of her academic daughter's lazy but endearing character. The way I remember it, the kitchen was warm and steamy, and we both had a good time in our own very different ways.

Last Christmas, I invited eleven friends for a traditional Ukrainian Christmas Eve meal. This is a complicated ritual meal with twelve dishes. One year, I tried to do it all myself, the way my mother does. I shopped, prepped, cooked, and cleaned for three solid days. I was faint with exhaustion, and rigid with resentment by the time the first guest arrived. I watched my friends eat my dinner with grim detachment. My culture felt like an artifact, like something on display.

Since then, I have changed my ways. I email the invited guests with a list of the ritual dishes, placing asterisks next to the ones they may choose to make or purchase. Then there's usually a flurry of emails and phone calls as my friends vie to score the easily purchased dishes, like *challah* bread or poppy seed roll. Recipes are sent to those brave enough to attempt borscht, fruit compote, or green beans with prunes. The three dozen *varennyky* are assigned for purchase to someone with a car, along with very specific instructions on the exact deli in the particular Polish or Ukrainian neighbourhood they must journey to, the terminology they must use, and the way to store them before the dinner.

My friends pretend to complain about the exacting nature of this dinner, and the stress that accompanies their trip to the deli or the Jewish bakery, places they may never have visited before. There are always stories to tell: the harrowing process of making sugar syrup for the compote, and the terrifying way it solidified in the fridge; the formidable ladies who work the counter at the Polish deli on Roncesvalles, with their thick, strong arms and impatient glares. Someone pours me a glass of wine as I lean against the kitchen counter, listening. This ritual is now owned by all of us.

This year, my friend Terri was assigned the simple task of going to Praha, a very good Czech deli in Toronto, to obtain the *varennyky*. She called me two days before the meal.

"I haven't made it to Prague, or Pravda, or whatever it's called. I might just go to the supermarket instead. I think Loblaws has perogies on sale."

[Shocked silence on my end.]

"Or," she continued, cunningly, "I could make them."

"What?" I sputtered. "Don't be ridiculous! It takes the average Ukrainian woman thirty years to learn how to make them! And you're … you're English!" I took on a martyr's tone. "Look, never mind. I have a million things to do. And there's a storm warning. But I'm sure I can bicycle to Praha and get them myself."

"It might interest you to know," she continued, undaunted, "that I've done research."

"Research? Is this a Master's thesis? Are we conducting a seminar?"

"Well," she said, defiantly, "I have. I looked at seventy-two different recipes on the Internet. I am going to make *varennyky* from the Transcarpathian region." She pronounced it *Transcarpah-thian*.

"Transcar-*paye*-thian," I said, correcting her haughtily.

"Whatever," she said. "I'm making them, and you can't stop me." And with that, she hung up.

I wondered if I should have a backup plan, or just cancel the dinner entirely. Without properly-made *varennyky*, the meal would have no centre, would be a fake. Terri phoned me again with an update: according to Transcarpathian custom she was sealing the edges of the dough shut with the tines of a fork. This almost took me over the edge. I had never heard of such a thing. I warned her that if she went through with the fork thing—dire tragedy, including the unsealing of the *varennyky* in the boiling water—would ensue.

I flew to my mother's city on Christmas Day. I couldn't wait to tell the Transcarpathian perogy story to the Divas of the Church. A few days after Christmas, I wrangled an invitation to one of their lugubrious, pastry filled tea parties. I told them about the indignities of Internet research, the frightening prospect of unsealed dough, the sleepless nights I endured as a result. They made vague *tsk*ing sounds while I scarfed down as many of their pastries as I could manage. Mouth full of poppyseed roll, I mentioned the fork thing. I was sure they'd be up in arms about the fork thing.

But in the end, they all took Terri's side. "You don't go to a store to buy *varennyky*, no matter how good they are," said one of the Divas in a somewhat admonitory tone. (Clearly she'd been told the story about my slatternly perogy-making behaviour.) "Transcarpathia was once part of Ukraine, you know," said another, rather smugly, I thought. "My sister-in-law's father is buried there. They have beautiful wooden churches."

"Hmph. Using a fork. Very different. I wouldn't mind seeing her recipe," said my Ma, with what seemed like grudging admiration in her voice.

And with that, the Divas moved on to much more important matters, like who had died recently, what food had been served at the funeral, and how it compared with another funeral three weeks earlier. Everyone had a round of peach schnapps. I settled in. The conversation turned to the way they had all met, the girlish pranks they played on each other, the gorgeous hairdos and flashy dresses they used to wear. I eyed my mother: she giggled as she listened, and for a moment, I had a glimpse of the mischievous young girl she'd once been.

Languages change with time. So do traditions.

Terri's *varennyky* weren't at all like my mother's. They didn't unseal. Everyone loved them. Terri had poured all of her generosity and artistic talent into their making. They were delicious, but they had a unique texture and taste. Perhaps that was the point. Authentic words, authentic rituals—they're as slippery as a *varennyk* in boiling water.

TERRI'S TRANSCARPATHIAN VARENNYKY

Loosely based on a recipe from Favorite Recipes Collected by St. Mary's Ladies Guild *by Imogene Citrak*.

Have all ingredients at room temperature. (Just sit all the ingredients on the kitchen table and tune in to whatever is on the radio for half an hour while you set a cauldron of water to boil, bring out 3 bowls, a big pastry or cutting board, measuring cups and spoons, some clean tea towels, a couple of cookie trays, a big serving plate and spoon.)

Prepare the filling first:
1 tbsp onion, grated
2 tbsp butter
1 cup old cheddar cheese, grated
2 cups mashed potatoes
Salt and pepper to taste

Mix the onion, butter, and cheese into the warm mashed potatoes. Add salt and pepper to taste. The filling should be thick enough to hold its shape.

Then make the dough. In a bowl, toss and mix:

3 cups flour
½ tsp salt

Make a big, floury mound on the pastry board, dig out a well, and pour in the following mixture in 4 parts, each time tossing the floury edges into the middle with a fork, until the mass is kneadable:

1 cup whole milk, warmed
5 tbsp sour cream

2 tbsp butter, melted

Knead the dough for 5 minutes, sparingly, then place in a bowl covered with a clean tea towel to sit for 10 minutes, until medium-soft. Divide the dough into 4 parts and roll out one at a time while leaving the other balls covered in the warm bowl. Roll dough very thin, about 1/8-inch, and use a wide mouth jar to cut out circles about 3 inches in diameter.

Place a dough circle in your palm and press a spoonful of filling onto one half of the circle. Then fold the other half over the filling and place it on the floured board. Close the edges firmly with the tines of a fork. (Sometimes you have to wet the edge to make it stick, or use a little whisked egg white as glue. But you have to seal them completely or the filling squishes out when they boil.) Dust the varennyky with flour. Place the finished pieces onto a clean tea towel so they won't stick to the plate or pan, and then cover them with a second clean tea towel to prevent drying too much.

Drop about 6 varennyky at a time into a large quantity of rapidly boiling salted water for 3–4 minutes. Stir very gently to prevent sticking to bottom or each other. They will become puffy and float to the surface when they are ready. Use a slotted spoon to remove them. Drain in a colander. Place into a wide-bottomed serving dish and sprinkle with melted butter. Gently shift them to distribute butter so they don't stick to each other.

Serve warm, with sour cream and sautéed onions on the side.

APPLES

I used to live in an apartment with an apple tree in the backyard that bore fruit every two years. I grew to appreciate this
tree's sense of restraint, its measured creativity, its ability to
leave me wanting more.

Apples may be the plain jane of fruits, but there is nothing
as elegant as a good, flaky *galette de pomme* from a French
patisserie, washed down with a cup of espresso. Few drinks
are as refreshing as a tart, sparkling apple cider on a hot day.
Apples are the language of the people, of common speech: *apple of my eye, apple-cheeked, motherhood and apple pie.*

When I was seven years old, my family spent a year in
England. Those were good times, as I recall; my professor father was on sabbatical and had extra time to spend with us.
This seemed to make Mama happier: the flickering home movies and faded snapshots record that she laughed more often,
and wore her hair in a Jackie Kennedy flip that I adored. I
liked having *Tato* around, wearing his shabby weekend clothes
all the time, making us breakfast *and* lunch, brooding in the
study, puttering in the garden. It didn't matter what we did
together, it just mattered that he was there. But my father, as
if to make up for all the previous absences, planned a year's
worth of Sunday tourist events for us: the Tower of London,
the British Museum, Madam Tussaud's, Buckingham Palace.
After church, and before the scheduled museum or gallery visit,

we would have a picnic in London's Hyde Park, rain or shine. The rationale behind these no-frills lunches was undoubtedly to save money; nonetheless, I loved those damp, grassy *al fresco* meals more than anything else we would do that day. We lounged on striped canvas chairs that were strewn around the park, and ate the liverwurst or kolbassa sandwiches on rye bread that my mother had prepared early that morning, accompanied by tea from Thermos flasks. Everything had a different flavour that year: those liverwurst sandwiches, spiced with the novelty of downtown London, were oddly delicious, and the tea, flavoured with lemon and sugar, made an unusually smooth and silky passage down the throat.

It seemed too that the apples in England had a deeper, richer flavour. I remember that there were apple trees everywhere, all the apples you could possibly want, apples for free. There were red apples with pink, fleshy insides, magically nestled in a hedge outside the elementary school I attended. Gnarled old apple trees could be found in the commons behind our house, proffering golden russet fruits with a nectar-like taste that even now I associate with the woodsmoke-and-diesel smell of London in the fall. Our neighbour, a greengrocer with grimy hands and a gracious smile, would bring us brown paper bags of apples from his shop, and Mama would make him sit down and have tea and sponge cake while he spoke to us of apples.

In the spring of that sabbatical year, my parents took us to the continent: five children and two adults, and all of our emotions and desires, crammed inside a blue Fiat. My memories from that trip are piecemeal: I have several mental images of the Fiat, stalled and smoking by the side of the road. The family album confirms that my mother was far less cheerful than usual during that three-week period. I remember evenings in small Italian towns, our little car grunting and labouring up and down hills under dark blue skies, and stopping in front of dingy *pensions* with flashy neon signs as my father went in to negotiate a price for a family with *cinque bambini* (five children). More often than not he would return to tell my mother that we couldn't afford the place while she stared straight ahead, her mouth a grim, faded pink lipstick line. When we finally found a hotel that fit the budget, we usually all slept in the same room. In the morning, we'd have a breakfast of bread, triangles of processed cheese, and the inevitable Thermos of sweet tea. All my mother remembers of those rented rooms are grey, threadbare sheets and the distinct possibility of bed bugs. She says she often slept in her clothes. I remember only how the fresh baguette crunched pleasingly in my mouth, and how pretty those triangles of cheese were, with their colourful pictures of little Swiss girls posed in front of mountains, and their gold tin foil.

There were so many things I tasted for the first time on that trip: salad that was little more than a bowl of green leaves, dressed with a splash of vinegar and dash of olive oil, each condiment in its own corked glass carafe. Raspberry gelato. Freshly made spaghetti with a simple *pomodoro* sauce and grated *parmigiano*, no relation to the yellow powder we poured out of a box back home. I was only seven but I remember the smell of espresso, cigarettes, and fresh croissant on the streets of Paris the day we went to see the Eiffel Tower.

I realize now that my parents were working with the most meagre of budgets, and that my father, on that trip, gave me a lasting lesson: how to travel and eat with moderation and elegance. Those were still the days of the Iron Curtain, and my refugee father, with a wife and family, could not risk going back to Ukraine from which he might never return. This was as close as he could get to Eastern Europe, as much as he could show us of where he was from. For a small child from Alberta, this was distilled down to a series of simple but unforgettable film frames: old stone buildings with terracotta roofs; roads that wound through fields of lavender and groves of poplar; fresh, simple, country food. And also Paris, Geneva, Rome, Milan, Venice: some of the world's greatest cities, seen through a child's eyes, from the crowded windows of a little blue car.

Years later, as an adult, I returned to Europe to screen a film in Amsterdam. After the film festival was over, and with an itch to explore, I took a train by myself to Berlin. It was November, and November in Berlin is a grim time. Every word of German I heard resonated with history, with my father's history, with the camps. In the autumn gloom, all I could see were the bullet holes in the Reichstag; the cold, wide expanses of Alexanderplatz; the empty spaces where buildings stood and people thrived, before the war. The Berlin Wall had come down only a year earlier, but there were still long painful scars of rubble and dust to mark where it had stood. There was also a silence in those places that hadn't been there before. With one step, I could walk through the Iron Curtain that had separated my father from his past for so many decades.

I roamed like a ghost back and forth across that invisible wall. I visited the Checkpoint Charlie Museum, which houses an odd collection: artifacts of various escapes across the Berlin Wall, from east to west. There were photographs of a man who spent a year shovelling an underground tunnel, and of a woman who packed herself inside a suitcase—the suitcase was there, on display. Afterwards, I met up with a woman named Madeleine, in a high-ceilinged café across the street from the museum. I ordered *apfelkuchen mit schlagesahne*—apple cake with whipped cream—and a dense, bracing cup of espresso. We talked about the exhibits. "It shows the creativity of escape," said Madeleine, in that simple, brilliant way of speaking that all Berliners seemed to have. "But this museum, what it shows and what it doesn't show, is also a problem."

Later in the day, I went to the train station to buy tickets and stow my luggage for the night train back to Amsterdam and my flight home. As I was trying to decode the locker system, I met two black men from France, en route to St Petersburg. They told me in French that they had been studying in Russia for a year. I asked them what it was like for black people in Russia and this elicited a torrent of information I only half-understood: harassment on the streets, poverty, a Soviet tradition of divisiveness and individuality preventing the formation of activist movements. The men hoped to start an underground journal of black literature once they returned to Russia. We exchanged addresses and shook hands before they ran to catch their train.

Half an hour later, as I was standing in line for my ticket, I heard the sound of splintering glass. I turned to look: a group of skinheads had thrown a beer bottle in the direction of an Afro-German man. No one said anything, no one reacted. Including me.

One's sense of home is always relative. Living on the ground floor of that tottering, dark, wood-shingled house in Vancouver, I saw three apple harvests, representing five years that I stayed in the same place, a very long time for me. The apple tree's roots became my own, if only for a time.

But home is also in relation to what is *not* home; we define ourselves by what we *aren't*, identity forming itself along that slippery, uncomfortable edge. The shrill sound of splintering glass echoing through the Berlin train station locates me within the uneasy privileges of race. The clipped cadences of a skinhead's German epithets pulls me back to my father's imprisonment. The taste of *apfelkuchen* takes me home, to my mother's kitchen and the apple strudel she used to make from scratch, beating the dough against the table so hard we thought she was mad about something, then stretching it so thin you could see through it.

And home is also this: the thin, barely visible underpainting of grief and loss. Bleached-out flashes of film frames. The exact timbre of my brother Roman's voice, heard as though via a film's scratchy old soundtrack. The smell of kasha on a winter morning, and my father's joyful, achingly dependable, wake-up call.

When I first intuited the news of my father's death, I felt a strange nothingness. I was at Coupe Bizarre, a hair stylist on Queen Street West in Toronto, the year I was completing my Master's degree. Krys was getting her hair cut by Jimi Imij, our favourite transgendered hairdresser. I picked up my messages, shrill and repetitious: *call home, call home.* I didn't want to interrupt Krys's haircut, which was going so well. I ran across the street to a dim beerhall inhabited by raging crack whores. There was a payphone beside the bar. I called my mother. She slowly arranged Ukrainian words in order over the flickering telephone line. Later, I would use those words again and again: pluck them out of my eardrums where they vibrated tunelessly, and place them in the space between my lover and me, my best friend and me, my therapist and me. My. Father. Has Died. Lingering in the beerhall, I immediately ordered a double Scotch. And a huge plate of nachos, all dressed.

I became terribly, insatiably hungry. The next day, I took a train from Toronto to Ottawa, for the memorial service. It was fall. Trees scorched red and orange stood in relief against an uncertain, pockmarked sky. The cheese and roasted eggplant sandwich Krys had so carefully packed barely made a dent. At my mother's house I fell gratefully, greedily, upon the food. There was potato salad and marinated carrots. There were cabbage rolls, roast ham, rye bread. There were pastries and torte provided by the Divas of the Church, stuff you can rarely buy anywhere, anymore: sour cherry squares, poppyseed roll, apple cake. The food made sense; nothing else did. My brothers watched nervously as I had one, two, then three helpings, followed by torte, and pastry, and coffee. The house was full of friends and family and resonating with sound. When my father was alive, he always led the conversations: pockets of silence filled the spaces between his ponderous words and lengthy sighs. But on that day, distant cousins spoke to one another, saying witty, generous things. I met my cousin's wife Lida for the first time, even though I'd known her most of my life. I noticed she had dark brown x-ray eyes: she could see how hungry and how sad I was.

I have had to create a complicated riddle in my head: *If I missed my father, what would I miss?* My father, you see, was not an easy man. He believed in a myth of genius, which meant that he saw himself as being of the world, and belonging only incidentally to his family. He was often argumentative or harshly critical. As an adult, I see how those things mark my life, like a tongue running over and over the place where a missing tooth once grew. Daughter of a demanding, traumatized man, I have chosen lovers in my father's image again and again: moody and vain; brilliant, worldly, and charming.

But a daughter's love is like a phantom limb. Cut off at the root, it insinuates itself just the same. *If I missed my father, what would I miss?*

Among all the delicious things my father used to purchase at the market there was one, to my child-like sensibilities, truly horrible thing. *Salo. Salo* is fat. Pig's fat, to be exact. It's soft, white, and glistening: bacon, really, *sans* the meaty red stripes. As soon as he got home from the market, my father would release his precious slab of *salo* from its shiny, grease-stained butcher's paper, cutting off thin slices and putting them into his mouth. "Ahhh, delicious," he'd say, like it was caviar. "You don't know what you're missing." We kids would inflate our cheeks, pretending to suppress an attack of vomiting. But even though it was completely legitimate, by every known standard of every Canadian kid you knew, to say that *salo* was totally gross, your revulsion got transformed into something odd, then and there, and my dad's weird un-Canadian behaviour became the most sophisticated thing in the world.

In a way, I miss that about my father, too.

The story of mourning my father begins and ends with food. No matter how austere the mood in the house, there was always food. There was always a pause, to have dinner, or to sample some cheese. There were always Polish honey cookies and knishes, and *hamantaschan*; there was always pumpernickel bread, kolbassa, and German mustard; we never lacked for Hungarian jam, Turkish *halvah*, green grapes, Granny Smith apples, and oranges; there was always wine, there was always food. We came together, isotopes towards a nucleus, at dinnertime, conversation exploding over the food. My father, stern and rotund at the head of the table, made us talk of culture and politics as we ate; my mother softened prickly debates and hardened attitudes with food so terribly delicious it silenced us for moments at a time. I identified too strongly with my mother, who always hovered like a shadow behind the kitchen counter, rarely sitting down with us. My brothers' and my father's opinions raged and percolated, while I rose above them and observed, like a film camera on a crane. A brown, oval-shaped faux wood-grain kitchen table, piled with *varennyky*, chicken stew, an iceberg lettuce salad, a plate of sliced rye bread. Six children slouched in vinyl chairs, a dad, so present, at the head of the table, a mom, at the stove, dishing out food that had taken hours to make; food that contained more creativity, love, and loss than we could possibly imagine.

Presence and absence, both. Eating, that was about fullness and emptiness. *Wanting more*, that ineffably human trait, that gene passed on from my father to me. A hunger that drove him across continents, and accompanies me like a delightful yet narcissistic companion through the years.

And sometimes, the piercing knowledge—precious and rare as the capricious taste of blood oranges in February, or an apple in the fall with perfect, mouth-tingling tartness—that what you have is enough.

Marusya Bociurkiw is a filmmaker, food blogger, and author of three previous books, including the novel *The Children of Mary* and the short story collection *The Woman Who Loved Airports*. She has read and performed her work in Canada, the US and Europe, and on CBC radio. She has been producing films and videos in Canada for the past fifteen years including, most recently, *Flesh and Blood: A Journey Between East and West*. She has a PhD in Interdisciplinary Studies and currently lives in Toronto, where she teaches media studies.